"Mark O'Keefe gives us a con
thought of Teresa of Avila and
directors and spiritual directio
new to the practice of direction and for those long experienced in
giving or receiving it. *Learned, Experienced, and Discerning*
witnesses to how contemporary practice benefits by drawing from
the classic works of these two Carmelite reformers."

> —Raymond Studzinski, OSB
> School of Theology and Religious Studies
> The Catholic University of America

"A masterful exploration of the contributions of two Carmelite
'doctors of the church' to the understanding and practice of
spiritual guidance, in their own time and ours. Gathering and
skillfully explaining key passages, O'Keefe both focuses on and
exemplifies the three interconnected qualities that Teresa of Avila
and John of the Cross consider 'essential in a good spiritual
director,' namely, learning, experience, and prudence (or
discernment). This book is a wonderful and very readable resource
for contemporary spiritual directors and those they serve."

> —Steven Payne, OCD, author of *The Carmelite Tradition:
> Spirituality in History*

Learned, Experienced, and Discerning

St. Teresa of Avila and St. John of the Cross on Spiritual Direction

Mark O'Keefe, OSB

LITURGICAL PRESS
Collegeville, Minnesota

www.litpress.org

Cover design by Monica Bokinskie. Statues of Saint John of the Cross and Saint Teresa of Avila, Plaza de las Carmelitas, Spain. Photos courtesy of Wikimedia Commons (CC-BY-SA 2.0).

1   2   3   4   5   6   7   8   9

Library of Congress Cataloging-in-Publication Data

Names: O'Keefe, Mark, 1956– author.
Title: Learned, experienced, and discerning : St. Teresa of Avila and St. John of the Cross on spiritual direction / Mark O'Keefe, OSB.
Description: Collegeville, Minnesota : Liturgical Press, [2020] | Includes bibliographical references. | Summary: "Insights into the qualities that should mark a good spiritual director-learned, experienced, and discerning-as demonstrated by the spiritual texts of Teresa of Avila and John of the Cross"— Provided by publisher.
Identifiers: LCCN 2019055214 (print) | LCCN 2019055215 (ebook) | ISBN 9780814688106 (paperback) | ISBN 9780814688342 (epub) | ISBN 9780814688342 (mobi) | ISBN 9780814688342 (pdf)
Subjects: LCSH: Spiritual direction—Catholic Church. | Spiritual directors. | Carmelites—Spiritual life. | Teresa, of Avila, Saint, 1515-1582. | John of the Cross, Saint, 1542-1591.
Classification: LCC BX2350.7 .O54 2020 (print) | LCC BX2350.7 (ebook) | DDC 253.5/3—dc23
LC record available at https://lccn.loc.gov/2019055214
LC ebook record available at https://lccn.loc.gov/2019055215

Contents

Acknowledgments

This work began at the suggestion of Dr. Robert Alvis, academic dean at Saint Meinrad Seminary and School of Theology, where I am privileged to serve on the faculty. I am grateful to him for his encouragement and to my faculty colleagues for their collegial support. The Spanish-language research for the project was conducted in the excellent library of the Centro Internacional Teresiano Sanjuanista (Universidad de la Mística) in Avila, Spain. I am grateful to the staff there for their support and friendship. Fr. J. Lawrence Richardt, a priest of the Archdiocese of Indianapolis, kindly read over and made suggestions that have improved this text. But I am especially grateful to Larry for the many years that he has served as my own spiritual director through a journey with inevitable twists and turns. He is, in my experience—and that of many others, I am sure—a truly learned, experienced, and discerning director. With great respect and heartfelt appreciation for his ministry, I dedicate this book to him.

Translations and Abbreviations

All quotations from the works of Teresa of Avila are taken from *The Collected Works of St. Teresa of Avila*, translated by Kieran Kavanaugh, OCD, and Otilio Rodriguez, OCD, 3 vols. (Washington, DC: ICS Publications, 1976–1985, 1987, 2012).

The following abbreviations will be used in references to Teresa's works:

F = *The Book of Her Foundations*

L = *The Book of Her Life*

M = *Meditations on the Song of Songs*

W = *The Way of Perfection*

IC = *The Interior Castle*

LE = Letters

S = *Soliloquies*

ST = *Spiritual Testimonies*

References to particular texts within these works is indicated in the following way:

For the first four works, the first number refers to the chapter, and the second number refers to the paragraph. Thus, W 3.5 refers to *The Way of Perfection*, chapter 3, paragraph 5.

Regarding *The Interior Castle*, the first number refers to the dwelling place, the second number refers to the chapter, and the third number refers to the paragraph. Thus, IC 3.4.2 refers to the third dwelling place, chapter 4, paragraph 2.

All quotations from the works of John of the Cross are taken from *The Collected Works of St. John of the Cross*, rev. ed., translated by Kieran Kavanaugh, OCD, and Otilio Rodriguez, OCD (Washington, DC: ICS Publications, 1991).

The following abbreviations will be used in references to John's works:

A = *The Ascent of Mount Carmel*

C = *The Spiritual Canticle*

F = *The Living Flame of Love*

L = *Letters*

N = *The Dark Night*

Pre = *The Precautions*

SLL = *The Sayings of Light and Love*

References to particular texts within these works is indicated in the following way:

For *The Ascent of Mount Carmel* and *The Dark Night*, the first number indicates the book, the second number refers to the chapter, and the third number indicates the paragraph.

For example: A 2.3.4 would refer to the *Ascent*, book two, chapter 3, paragraph 4.

In a similar manner, for *The Spiritual Canticle* and *The Living Flame of Love*, the first number refers to the stanza and the second number to the paragraph. Thus, C 3.4 is a reference to the commentary on stanza 3, paragraph 4 of *The Spiritual Canticle*.

Introduction

Learned, experienced, and discerning (discreet, prudent)—these are the three characteristics that both St. Teresa of Avila[1] and St. John of the Cross emphasize as essential in a good spiritual director. Although they lived in sixteenth-century Spain, they have a great deal to contribute to our own age in which there is an abundance of writing about spiritual direction, programs to form spiritual directors, many Christians who are seeking it out, and many, many more who could certainly benefit from it.

Teresa and John were Carmelites—Teresa, the courageous visionary who began the Discalced reform, and John, her close collaborator in this work. They were both mystics and teachers of prayer. They were both writers about prayer and about the broader Christian journey toward union with God. Their written works are classics of Western Christian spirituality and mysticism, and their descriptions, definitions, and analyses have continued to form the thought of virtually all those who

1. Although widely and popularly known as Teresa of Avila, the name that she took at the beginning of the Discalced reform and by which she referred to herself was Teresa of Jesus.

have subsequently pondered and written about similar topics and experiences. Today, they are both recognized as Doctors of the Church—their writings rightly promoted as full of reliable and insightful teaching into the spiritual journey for all of their readers throughout the ages.

But Teresa of Avila and John of the Cross were not recluses, withdrawn solitaries who retreated to silent cloisters where they wrote obscure and wonderful mystical treatises. They were a flesh-and-blood woman and man who were called and gifted to assist other ordinary human beings to walk along the extraordinary path through which God had led them. They themselves experienced spiritual direction, and they themselves were spiritual guides for others. It is true that their sixteenth-century writings can sometimes seem to contemporary readers to be either chatty, mystical travelogues in the case of Teresa's texts or like austere ascetical manuals or abstract academic treatises on mysticism in the case of John's works. But their purpose is ultimately practical and ministerial—to help their fellow Christians to walk the way that leads to union with God by learning to be open, docile, and also utterly determined to know and embrace God's sometimes mysterious but always loving will.

Teresa and John share a broad sense of what spiritual direction is, what is essential in a good director, and the attitudes that will be most helpful in those who seek the spiritual companionship of another. They have, of course, their own emphases, their own ways of saying things, and undoubtedly their own personal experience of direction. In the chapters that follow, we will examine both their shared viewpoints as well as their distinctive emphases.

It must be noted that our purpose is not to lay out a general exposition of the teachings of Teresa of Avila and John of the Cross about prayer and the Christian life. That would be a very worthy project but well beyond our focus here. If readers already possess some general knowledge and familiarity with their writings, it will likely help them to grasp more quickly the specific points being made by Teresa and John about spiritual direction. But, for our purposes here, such prior familiarity is not essential—though I would count it as a profitable outcome if, having read this book, the reader would feel drawn to pick up the works of Teresa and John for themselves.

Our study will proceed as follows: an introductory part will offer general remarks about spiritual direction itself as it is understood today, looking briefly both at a broad working definition and the terminology used to describe it. A chapter on the pertinent context for Teresa's and John's writings on the topic of direction will help to distinguish their lasting contribution from what is simply a reflection of their own times and to understand their unique perspectives. The second part will look at Teresa of Avila as a recipient of spiritual direction, what she learned about what constitutes a good spiritual director, her own witness as a director for others, and a sense of her holistic spirituality as the subject matter of direction. The third part will examine John of the Cross as a spiritual director, some of his general thoughts on direction, and what constitutes both bad and good directors. Although Teresa and John reach the same basic conclusions about the essential qualities in a spiritual guide, it is useful to look at the thought of each separately, knowing that some readers may have more interest in one than the other. The particular thought of each, in any case, is worthy of individual study. A final chapter will very briefly draw together the insights that they offer for contemporary reflections on spiritual direction and especially on spiritual directors themselves.

In many places, I will be quoting the works of these two Carmelite Doctors of the Church at some length. This work is not, by any means, intended as a mere collection of excerpts from their writings with some commentary to provide explanations. But, as the reader will see, their own words often express more directly and powerfully—and sometimes with far more charm—the point under consideration than any paraphrase or analysis of them could do. One sees more clearly that their purpose is practical and ministerial, seeking to offer real assistance to those who feel in need of solid spiritual guidance or who feel called to serve as a spiritual companion to others.

Part One

Preliminary Considerations

Before we examine more directly what Teresa of Avila and John of the Cross have to say about spiritual direction, we begin by looking at the lens that we will apply to our study. When we speak of their view on spiritual direction, how do we understand today what the term "spiritual direction" means? From our contemporary perspective, what does the relationship of director and directee involve? Our starting point will influence what we are looking for in their writings and what we choose to highlight. On the other hand, our own contemporary understanding of the topic can be expanded or clarified by what we find. In fact, I will suggest that this is precisely the case.

These two Carmelite Doctors of the Church wrote what have become spiritual classics whose insights transcend their own particular audience and time. And yet, what we are examining from our contemporary perspective involves what

1

was formulated and written for a people of another time and culture. Without some understanding of the distinctive world in which Teresa and John lived and wrote, we might misunderstand what they are trying to express in their own terms and with their particular emphases.

Chapter One

What Is Spiritual Direction?

If we are to speak of the spiritual direction in the thought of Teresa of Avila and John of the Cross, we should offer some general sense of what we mean by the term. In fact, in our day, we must first begin by asking about the usefulness of the term itself.

What to Call It?

Many contemporary authors have grown uncomfortable with the term "spiritual direction." First, to use the adjective "spiritual" can seem to suggest that the relationship is focused too narrowly on a person's "spiritual life"—that is, to prayer and one's interior relationship with God. Today, there is a greater sense of the Christian life as holistic. Our prayer exists in the wider context of our daily living and relationships. Even our relationship with God is not solely about explicit moments of prayer or simply a one-to-one relationship with the divine. Our life as Christians

3

and our relationship with God does, of course, involve prayer, but they are broader. Therefore, the subject matter of what we call spiritual direction must also be broader. On the other hand, the relationship is essentially focused on the presence, action, and guidance of the Holy Spirit in the life of the person; in that sense, it might be called "spiritual."

Also problematic is the term "direction," because it seems to suggest some lessening or limiting of the personal discernment, freedom, and initiative of the person who seeks out a guide. It seems to suggest that the so-called director is actively handing out instructions or even laying out a plan of action rather than helping the person to discern God's action in his or her individual life. Contemporary authors emphasize that the relationship traditionally called spiritual direction is not about authoritatively directing another—and certainly not along a preset and generic "spiritual" path. It is not a matter of teaching spiritual principles or giving advice or counsel. On the other hand, the relationship traditionally called spiritual direction does involve "directing" the other person's attention to the movement of the Spirit in his or her life. If the Christian life is a like a journey, we are heading in a "direction," and guides, maps, and signs can keep us on the move and heading in the "right" direction.[1]

---

1. Gordon T. Smith acknowledges the concerns with the term "direction," but he also cautions that there may be too much resistance to the term and to the notion of spiritual "authority" and freely chosen accountability to another. Even a word like "pastor" is also open to critique—suggesting to some that the people are too dumb to know their

As a consequence of these concerns, other terms are now being suggested and used: spiritual friendship, companionship, or accompaniment. The last mentioned is frequent in contemporary Spanish literature in relationship to Teresa and John: *acompañamiento* (accompaniment) and *acompañante* (companion). We might also speak of spiritual guidance and a spiritual guide (though this may still suggest, to some, too much focus on the initiative of the so-called guide) or perhaps of spiritual mentoring (though this term may seem to focus too much on some particular skill set). Looking to the ancient desert tradition, we might use the terms spiritual "father" or "mother" (though this might suggest that the person who comes for guidance remains a kind of child in relation to the guide). Protestant Evangelical literature speaks of "shepherding" or "discipling."

In the end, recognizing that there are problems with the term "spiritual direction" and acknowledging that alternatives exist, William Barry and William Connolly in the revised edition of their classic work on spiritual direction opt to continue using the traditional term. They conclude that it remains the most traditional and widely used term. As such, at least its general meaning is immediately understood by readers—

---

way, in need of being corralled, and the like. Changing the name does not ultimately eliminate the cause for concern. Even so, direction is most usually done, he argues, by gentle nudging, urging, and suggesting (or, "with discretion," as Teresa and John would say it). Gordon T. Smith, *Spiritual Direction: A Guide to Giving and Receiving Direction* (Downers Grove, IL: InterVarsity Press, 2014), 11–12.

while the alternatives may require further explanation or clarification.[2] In the final analysis, any term has its limitations. And so, like Barry and Connolly, we will generally continue to use the terms "spiritual direction," "director," and "directee"—while alternating it with others, such as guidance and companionship, as general expressions of the same reality. Our purpose here is not to offer a definitive vocabulary and definition for the relationship traditionally called spiritual direction but rather to examine the experience and insights of Teresa of Jesus and John of the Cross.

What Teresa and John Called It

Neither John nor Teresa wrote about "spiritual direction" or "spiritual directors." Addressing largely the same reality in a different historical context, they simply use other terms. For Teresa, this involves, for the most part, only two terms used extensively. For John, there are a number of different terms. But their perspective on what we call spiritual direction, because of their historical and cultural world, is not exactly the same as ours, and the terms that they use reflect this difference.[3]

2. William A. Barry and William J. Connolly, *The Practice of Spiritual Direction*, 2nd ed. (New York: HarperOne, 2009), 10–11.

3. Janet Ruffing offers a historical overview of prevailing models of spiritual direction through the course of Church history. Janet Ruffing, *Uncovering Stories of Faith* (New York: Paulist Press, 1989), 2–17.

In Teresa's works, the person whom we might call a spiritual director is most frequently referred to as a "confessor."[4] In her day, only priests formally and openly offered spiritual guidance to others. And, as we will see, Teresa names many of the priests who served as her director-confessor over the years. Especially for cloistered nuns, it was the regular, scheduled arrival of a priest to hear the nuns' confessions that provided the easiest opportunity to seek spiritual counsel. Teresa certainly understood the difference between spiritual guidance and sacramental reconciliation. It seems likely that spiritual guidance was offered outside the actual confession and absolution of sin—though in the time set aside for the confessor to be present. It also appears that Teresa could speak of a spiritual guide as a "confessor" even when guidance did not occur in relation to a discrete moment of confession—that is, the person offering spiritual guidance was, on other occasions, a regular confessor. Thus, Teresa's use of the term "confessor" does not imply at all that she viewed spiritual direction as narrowly focused on the discussion of sin.

A second common term for Teresa (appearing especially in the *Life*) is *maestro*, usually translated as "master."[5] It is used

4. Her use of the term *confesor* is simply too frequent to list every occurrence. Note, for example, L 24.4, 7; 26.3–5; 33.1–4; W 5.1–6; IC 6.1.8; 6.6.2; 6.9.10–13. Note that the English translation may not always offer a literal translation of the Spanish word *confesor*.

5. See, for example, L 4.7, 9; 6.8; 13.3; 19.15; 23.8; 25.14; 40.8. Note that English translations may not provide a literal translation of the Spanish word *maestro*.

in the sense of a "spiritual master" or "master of the spiritual life," with the concomitant idea of having spiritual "disciples." It conveys a person with an acquired spiritual wisdom to share and, in that sense, a kind of teacher.

John of the Cross uses more varied terms for what we today might call a spiritual director. In the prologue of the *Ascent*, for example, he speaks of "guides/*guías*" (A Prol.3) and "spiritual fathers/*padres*" (A Pro.4) as well as a "confessor/*confesor*" (A Prol.6). His most frequent term is "spiritual master/*maestro espiritual*."[6] And concomitant with that term, he sometimes speaks of the person who seeks guidance as a "disciple/*discípulo*" (A 2.3.5; 2.18.1, 5–7; 2.19.11; 2.22.12; 3.45.3; F 3.30). Dennis Graviss concludes that the term "spiritual father" may come closest to describing John's sense of the role and stance of the spiritual guide.[7] But we also cannot ignore stronger connotations in John's use of terms like "govern"—in the *Ascent*, for example: "how their masters [*maestros*] ought to guide [*gobierna*]" (A 2.18.1) and "neither the soul nor its

6. Manuel Hódar Maldonado has found the term ten times in the *Ascent*, three times in the *Night*, and fifteen times in the *Flame* (*San Juan de la Cruz, guía de maestros espirituales: meta, camino, y guía del místico* [Burgos, Spain: Editorial Monte Carmelo, 2009], 153). Earlier in the same work (pp. 55–57), he reviews other terms and related verbs that John of the Cross uses to describe the relationship between the spiritual guide and the one who seeks guidance.

7. Dennis Graviss, *Portrait of the Spiritual Director in the Writings of Saint John of the Cross*, 2nd ed. (Rome, Italy: Edizioni Carmelitane, 2014), 112.

director [*quien la gobierna*]" (A 2.20.3). In the same text, he speaks of the spiritual guide as "the one whom God has destined to be spiritual judge over that soul [*quien Dios tiene puesto por juez espiritual de aquel alma*]" (A 2.22.16).

What we see in the terms used by both Teresa of Jesus and John of the Cross to name a spiritual guide—due largely, it could be argued, to the context in which they wrote—is an emphasis on teaching, guidance, and even shepherding. And yet, as we will see, both remain emphatic that the Holy Spirit is the true director and that the guide must attend to the individual person in his or her actual situation. And so, "spiritual accompaniment" or "companionship" would not be inappropriate terms to translate their meaning from the terms that they used in their day. Nor would the term "spiritual friendship" be out of place. Teresa famously defines prayer as a sharing between friends, and the task of the spiritual guide is to aid the person to grow in that relationship, including beyond times of explicit prayer. In fact, Teresa herself most often was or became a friend of those who directed her, and the letters of John of the Cross and the dedications of his prose commentaries also suggest the same.

What Is Spiritual Direction?

It is not our purpose—nor is it essential to our project—to arrive at a definitive contemporary definition of spiritual direction. Nonetheless, it is essential to offer at least a basic understanding of the nature of this relationship. One frequently quoted definition is offered by Barry and Connolly:

> We define Christian spiritual direction, then, as help given by
> one believer to another that enables the latter to pay attention
> to God's personal communication to him or her, to respond
> to this personally communicating God, to grow in intimacy
> with this God, and to live out the consequences of the
> relationship.[8]

They go on to insist that its subject matter is not only prayer but
life in general. Clearly the emphasis is on the action of God and
the person's relationship and communication with the divine.

Tilden Edwards offers a similar definition, likewise em-
phasizing that the principal focus of the relationship is the
Holy Spirit at work in the life of the person who comes for
guidance:

> The ministry of spiritual direction can be understood as the
> meeting of two or more people whose desire is to prayerfully
> listen for the movements of the Holy Spirit in all areas of the
> person's life (not just in their formal prayer life). It is a three-
> way relationship: among the *true* director who is the Holy
> Spirit (which in the Christian tradition is the Spirit of Christ
> in and among us), and the human director (who listens for the
> *directions* of the Spirit with the directee), and the directee.[9]

A final example, offered by Gordon T. Smith, highlights an
aspect of the relationship that would be particularly important
to John of the Cross—helping the person navigate transitions:

8. Barry and Connolly, *The Practice of Spiritual Direction*, 8.

9. Tilden Edwards, *Spiritual Director, Spiritual Companion: Guide to
Tending the Soul* (New York: Paulist Press, 2001), 2.

A *spiritual director* offers spiritual guidance and companionship to help us make sense of our faith journey, interpret with
us the significant markers on the road, and encourage us, particularly through the more difficult transitions and valleys of
our pilgrimage. Most of all, a spiritual director helps us make
sense of the witness of the Spirit—assisting us to respond well
to the question, "How is God present to me and how is God,
through the ministry of the Spirit, at work in my life?"[10]

Consistent with this definition (and resonating with what
Teresa and John will have to say), Smith goes on to offer five
essential characteristics of the good spiritual director. The
guide must (1) have a basic understanding of the theology of
the Christian life and particularly of the Holy Spirit (though
not necessarily based on formal academic training); (2) be
aware of the history of Christian spirituality in order to have
wisdom to offer those who come to them; (3) be compassion-
ate; (4) be present and attentive, both to the person and to the
Holy Spirit; and (5) be able to maintain confidentiality within
the deeper recognition that the sharing from and with the
person is itself a kind of sacred space.[11]

Divergence and Critique

Noting the terms used by Teresa and John above, we already
see that their understanding of spiritual direction is not completely in line with contemporary understandings. As we will

10. Smith, *Spiritual Direction*, 10; italics in original.
11. Smith, 82–86.

see, they are in complete agreement that the Holy Spirit is the true director, and they will emphasize that a good director must be discerning both of the Spirit's action and of the actual needs of the individual. But, at the same time, the terms that they use imply a greater emphasis on actual guidance, counsel, and even teaching offered by the director. As we will see, their particular historical and cultural context explains much of the difference in emphasis. But, at the same time, we must not too quickly dismiss the idea that their distinctive emphases may offer some amplification and even critique of current definitions.

Let us consider briefly, by way of example, some comments offered in the rightfully popular work of Barry and Connolly. These two contemporary authors insist that spiritual direction is not about "imparting directions for right living and right praying."[12] And if by that we mean that the director should not be offering conceptual, abstract, general teaching to those who come to them, this must certainly be true. Spiritual direction is not a class in spirituality, much less a workshop on prayer or good moral living. And yet, there is good reason that contemporary formation programs for spiritual direction generally offer and even require general introductions to the history of Christian spirituality and to its classic teachers. In direction, a person may be helped at particular moments by the introduction of wisdom from the tradition. This is not the same thing as some kind of teaching and prepackaged plan

12. Barry and Connolly, *The Practice of Spiritual Direction*, 143. See also 43.

imposed on a person's experience but rather the effort to enlighten the person's understanding of her or his own particular experience of the movements of the Spirit. We will see that John and Teresa both believe that a good director must be "learned"—not in order to offer general instruction or preset plans, but rather to be able to offer important guidance from proven sources of wisdom to discern the Spirit's directing.

Barry and Connolly, drawing on the traditional image of the Christian life as a journey and the director as a helper on that path, state:

> Spiritual direction is a helping relationship, but the help offered is more like that of a companion on a journey than of an expert who, before the journey begins, advises what roads to take and answers the traveler's questions. The companion tries to help the traveler read the maps, avoid dead ends, and watch out for potholes.[13]

Certainly, we can understand the published works of Teresa and John to be offering general road maps, answers to typical questions about the journey, and cautions about critical turns and potential pitfalls. But their understanding of spiritual direction does suggest being more than simply companions. One may surely benefit from walking with friends on any path, but on an arduous journey into the unknown, with many potential missteps, surely one wants an *expert* companion—an experienced and trained guide. For John and Teresa, knowledge and

13. Barry and Connolly, 145.

personal experience are both important in a director. They were well aware that every person's journey is unique and that, prior to that actual journey or apart from it, generic knowledge has limited value. But they believed that the traveler will be helped by those who have walked the same or a similar path before and who have studied well the available maps.

Finally, by way of suggesting that Teresa and John—even while acknowledging that their insights have to be adapted to contemporary realities—may be able to offer some challenge to current definitions of spiritual direction, we note the following comment of Barry and Connolly: "Thus, the only authority they [directors] can have is the authority of their own persons as people who belong to God and to God's people and who take seriously their own relationship to God and to God's people. As such, they are asked for help by other members of the community."[14] We can all certainly benefit from sharing our Christian journey and prayer with good friends who are people of genuine faith and committed to their own relationship with God and with the Christian community. But, surely, in a director, we want someone with a deeper foundation of personal and spiritual authority—not necessarily in any way formal, but lived experience of the journey, maturity in Christian practice, and some level of knowledge of the rich tradition that has grown up within that community of faith to which we and our directors belong. Teresa and John do expect such authority for anyone who answers a call to offer spiritual guidance to others.

14. Barry and Connolly, 145.

A contemporary spiritual author who bridges the understanding of contemporary writers and our two Carmelite authors is Thomas Merton. He was, of course, an avid student of both, and his brief reflection on spiritual direction reflects both contemporary and classic sensitivities (even if he does so in noninclusive terms):

> The director wants to know our inmost self, our *real* self. He wants to know us not as we are in the eyes of men, or even as we are in our own eyes, but as we are in the eyes of God. He wants to know the inmost truth of our vocation, the action of grace in our souls. His direction is, in reality, nothing more than a way of leading us to see and obey our real Director—the Holy Spirit, hidden in the depths of our soul. We must never forget that in reality we are not directed and taught by men, and that if we need human "direction" it is only because we cannot, without man's help, come into contact with that "unction (of the Spirit) which teaches us all things" (1 John 2:20).[15]

Merton points to themes that appear in the thought of Teresa of Jesus and John of the Cross—for example, the Holy Spirit as the true director, the presence of both God and our truest self "hidden" in the depths of our being (Merton's "Hidden Ground of Love" and Teresa's and John's "center of the soul"), and the need to bring together deepening prayer with overcoming self-deceit and illusory superficialities.

15. Thomas Merton, *Spiritual Direction and Meditation* (Collegeville, MN: Liturgical Press, 1960), 30.

Surely, all of the authors cited—especially Teresa of Avila and John of the Cross—would concur with the statement of Pope St. Gregory the Great in his *Pastoral Rule* (pt. 1, ch.1): "The direction/care of souls is the art of all arts" (*Ars artium cura animarum*).

Chapter Two

Insights in Context

A contemporary understanding of historical texts requires at least a basic grasp of their original context and intended audience. The works of Teresa of Avila and John of the Cross are no different. Although they have both been proclaimed Doctors of the Church and their writings acknowledged as true spiritual classics of the Christian tradition, they wrote in a particular time to a distinctive audience. Today's reader lives in a very different world than that of sixteenth-century Spain. Appreciating the enduring wisdom of Teresa and John about spiritual direction may require the ability to see beyond some of the particular emphases that made perfect sense in their own time but less so in our own.

In the present chapter, we will lay out briefly some important considerations for a contemporary understanding of their work: their historical (secular, ecclesial, and spiritual) context,[1]

---

1. For a more thorough study of Teresa and John's world, see my book *In Context: Teresa of Ávila, John of the Cross, and Their World* (Washington, DC: ICS Publications, 2020).

the thought of some of their contemporaries on spiritual direction, the three qualities of good spiritual guides in light of those circumstances, their intended audience, and their broader spiritual vision (some of which is viewed, by some, as perhaps problematic in our own age).

Spain in the Sixteenth Century

Sixteenth-century Spain was alive with a spirit of religious reform and spiritual fervor. Long before the formal inauguration of the Protestant Reformation, there were voices and movements of reform active throughout Europe. This was particularly true in Spain, where the monarchy was a major proponent of change: seeking the appointment of reform-minded bishops, promoting reform of the diocesan clergy and of religious orders, establishing universities with faculties of theology and biblical studies, and encouraging the publication of books of theology and spirituality. The printing press had only been invented in the previous century, but presses began to proliferate throughout Spain, publishing translations into the vernacular of classic and contemporary spiritual and mystical literature. Spain, only recently brought together from multiple kingdoms on the Iberian peninsula, welcomed scholars, ideas, and books from throughout Europe.

At the same time and related to these developments, within the general populace, there was a spiritual hunger for a deeper and more personal religion—beyond external rites and prayers and simple devotional practices. The so-called *Devotio Moderna* had arrived from northern Europe with its emphasis on a personal faith and relationship with Christ, the reading of Scripture in the vernacular, and deeper prayer. The reform of the religious orders had renewed their contemplative roots. Especially among the reformed Franciscans, there arose a type of prayer that they called the "prayer of recollection"—a form of quiet, wordless prayer that opened the person of prayer to the divine gift of contemplation.

But, at the same time, the sixteenth century was a time of widespread illiteracy. Even among the noble and wealthier classes, the inability to read was especially common among women. Teresa of Avila was an exception to this general rule. Books and their ideas could be shared orally, but access to such resources was limited for the vast majority of people. Coupled with the inability to read and difficulty of access to solid literature was the poor state of catechesis throughout the country. The reform of the clergy was not simply a matter of their own personal morality and spirituality. It was also intellectual and formational. In the period before the seminary system was established by the reforms of the Council of Trent, the average priest could have arrived at ordination by a kind of apprenticeship to a pastor without any formal theological training or even ability to understand the Latin of the liturgy. The sad state of catechesis was a reflection of the inadequate preparation of those who should have been able to promote and lead it.

It is no wonder that, in the particular context of the time, spiritual fervor and deep personal, spiritual experiences in prayer might lead to problems. Without a solid, basic understanding of Christian doctrine by which to understand and guide their experience, many of those who believed that they had enjoyed mystical encounter with God began to interpret their experience in heterodox ways. Different movements, under the general title of *alumbrados* ("enlightened ones"), developed—all of them sharing a tendency to deny the need for traditional Christian doctrine, ecclesial structures, or ritual practices. If one had attained a deep personal and secure relationship with God, what need would there be for doctrines, ecclesiastical hierarchies, sacraments, and external expressions of faith and piety? Joining those who may sincerely have believed in the authenticity of their divine encounters, there were also those who would later admit to being fakes and charlatans.

The Spanish Inquisition, originally founded as a national reality in order to ensure the orthodoxy of the large numbers of Jews and Muslims who had converted to Christianity in recent decades (many of them forced), became concerned about this rise of mystical experience and multiplication of claims of extraordinary mystical phenomena. The threat of the encroachment of Reformation ideas, which seemed cut from the same cloth as many of the tenets of *alumbrado* groups (though apparently without any direct connection between them), only heightened this concern. The general misogyny of the culture and the wider illiteracy among women (who could not seek a university education, even if they felt called to and capable of it) made them a special target of the inquisitors' concern. The result was a widespread and active suspicion of forms of prayer that promoted contemplation and the prohibition of books that taught it or seemed to seek to advance it (as well as vernacular translations of the Bible).

At the same time, a tension arose between those who had a formal, university-based learning (*letrados*) and those who had deep personal spiritual experience (*espirituales* or *experimentados*). The so-called learned often joined the Inquisition in its opposition to deeper prayer, while the so-called spirituals scoffed at the value of academic knowledge in matters of the life of the spirit and of deep personal faith. Of course, someone like John of the Cross could be both, and someone like Teresa could value both. They saw the need for spiritual directors to be both learned enough to keep people within the bounds of solid doctrine and, at least to some degree, experienced in the deeper paths of prayer that people were actively pursuing. At the same time, spiritual guides also had to be discerning enough to attend to the Holy Spirit and the needs of the individual person.

The Church throughout Europe in the sixteenth century was even more male-centered, hierarchical, and clerical than it is now. It was male clerics who could and did read, receive formal educations, and exercise authority. As we alluded to above, the culture in general held women largely in low esteem. While Teresa of Avila amazingly rose above and saw beyond these limited horizons—and, to some degree, criticized this reality—she was nonetheless formed by it and lived and wrote within it. In light of all of this, it is no wonder that both John and Teresa assumed that formal spiritual guides would be priests and that both would speak of the director's authority and the directee's obedience. Today, of course, we see that both women and men, laity and clerics, can serve as spiritual guides. While we might still acknowledge a certain personal, spiritual "authority" in the spiritual guide to whom we freely entrust the sharing of our journey as well as the openness that might constitute a kind of obedience (at least in the sense of the term's original meaning as listening), we see here a clear instance of the limitations of Teresa's and John's culturally bound perspectives.

Recognizing the Value of Spiritual Direction

Teresa of Avila and John of the Cross were not alone in their promotion of spiritual direction and in their sense of what their times demanded of good spiritual guides.[2] A brief look at the thought of just three of their contemporaries will help to place their perspectives into a context.

The first major published work of the burgeoning spiritual literature of sixteenth-century Spain appears to have been *The Exercises of the Spiritual Life* (*Ejercitatorio de la vida espiritual*) by the Benedictine abbot García Jiménez de Cisneros—a book of meditation that seems to have been read by and perhaps influenced Ignatius of Loyola. Cisneros was probably inspired by the Rule of Saint Benedict (46.5–6), which says: "When the cause of [a monk's] sin lies hidden in his conscience, he is to reveal it only to the abbot or to one of the spiritual elders, who know how to heal their own wounds as well as those of others, without exposing them and making them public."[3] The Spanish abbot urges the reader to seek out a "virtuous, disciplined, learned, mature" person who can provide consolation and example worthy of imitation and who can help them rise above half-heartedness and lack of sustained fervor.[4]

Francisco de Osuna's *Third Spiritual Alphabet* played a critical role in the early development of the mature spiritual

2. In this section, I am particularly indebted to Dennis Graviss, *Portrait of the Spiritual Director in the Writings of Saint John of the Cross*, 2nd ed. (Rome, Italy: Edizioni Carmelitane, 2014), 19–62.

3. Timothy Fry, ed., *The Rule of Saint Benedict 1980* (Collegeville, MN: Liturgical Press, 1981).

4. Quoted by Graviss, *Portrait of the Spiritual Director*, 23.

life of St. Teresa. Such was its diffusion in Spain at the time that it seems most likely that John of the Cross would have read it as well. By the time that Osuna published this work, the *alumbrados* had already become suspect. The Franciscans, who had promoted the prayer of recollection from which the *alumbrados* had developed their misguided notions, were actively distinguishing themselves from and criticizing the movement. It is no wonder that Osuna was a strong advocate of spiritual direction, recognizing that God remains the principal agent for growth in prayer and the Christian life. Wisdom born of experience, he writes, is the principal quality to be possessed by a sound spiritual guide. In fact, one of the treatises included in Osuna's work devotes a great deal of attention to spiritual direction.

John of Avila (not to be confused with John of the Cross) was one of the most widely known spiritual writers and figures of sixteenth-century Spain. It was to him that Teresa sent a draft of the *Book of Her Life* to ensure that the experiences about which she wrote were of divine origin. In his writings, John recommended seeking out a "guide and father" who possessed three essential qualities: learned, exercised (disciplined, mature in good habits/practices), and experienced. In fact, it would be dangerous, he cautioned, if the spiritual guide lacked any one of these characteristics.

The Three Qualities

We can conclude from the above that the identification of the three qualities of learning, experience, and discernment makes sense in light of the context and were not unique to

Teresa and John—though they bring them out with particular clarity and emphasis in the context of a wider spiritual wisdom. In the chapters that follow, we will look more closely at how their milieu formed Teresa and John in their particular reflections on these qualities. But before we move into the more particular studies of each, it may be useful to offer a brief summary of the impact of their times on their identification and reflection on these three essential characteristics as well as a few indications of the continued value of their insights.

A reliable spiritual guide must be *learned* in order to assist the person to interpret their own personal, spiritual experience in light of traditional Christian doctrine and scriptural truth. This was especially important in light of the mistaken paths taken by some of their contemporaries as well as to avoid the attention of the Inquisition. In our own age, as I will suggest in what follows, we may not need academic learning in the same way in order to offer helpful responses to the one coming for guidance, and yet, some foundational formation in theology, spirituality, and Scripture can provide a spiritual guide with a wealth of cautions, questions, challenges, and suggestions. We may not live in an age of mystical heresies, but the encroachment of New Age ideas, the tendency to think that "all religions are the same," and the reality of widespread subjectivism that tends to ignore what falls outside our own felt experience suggest the continued value of this quality, though understood in a contemporary way.

Teresa of Avila and John of the Cross were writing in a time of great spiritual fervor. Many sincere Christians seeking growth in prayer were walking into what seemed like largely uncharted territory. But with the promulgation of its Indices of Prohibited Books in 1551 and 1559, the Spanish Inquisition prohibited the publication of the majority of books on the topic of deeper prayer available to those who were hungry for such guidance. Besides learning, personal *experience* in the spiritual life came to be seen as essential to providing guidance to those seeking to enter into deeper prayer. Teresa herself reported having been harmed by those who advised her without having any experience of their own of the more mature journey of prayer. In our own day, "experience" may simply mean a personal commitment to and some maturity in the Christian life, having known personally the ups and downs, the difficulties, and the common paths of prayer.

Of the three qualities identified by Teresa and John, being *discerning* and prudent is perhaps the most immediately recognizable. Beyond learning and experience—and, at the same time, benefiting from and intertwined with them—the spiritual guide must be able to attend to the person in his or her actual situation and to the Holy Spirit, who authors, both contemporary and classic, agree is always the true director. Both a divine gift and a developed skill, discretion and discernment allow the spiritual director to move beyond academic learning and his or her own fundamentally personal experience to be truly present and attentive to another human person and to the Holy Spirit.

Their "Audience"

Teresa of Avila initiated the Discalced Carmelite reform during a time in which many religious orders were seeking a return to the original vision of their founders. Teresa—soon aided by

John of the Cross and others—founded what became the Discalced Carmelites, not because the Carmelites of their time were, in general, decadent or corrupt. But she did want a more radical return to the contemplative and even eremitical roots of the first Carmelite hermits who had banded together at Mount Carmel in the Holy Land in the twelfth century. Both Teresa and John, then, were writing especially for the zealous and fervent recent recruits to the Discalced reform, with its intense contemplative vision, and to their close lay friends and supporters. This fact helps to explain their often unabashed enthusiasm for moving forward with determination along the spiritual path. Their first readers and hearers would most probably have received the challenge with renewed enthusiasm of their own (though probably also in need of Teresa's and John's insistence on a steady determination through both dryness and consolation along the way). But we know that Teresa and John also had regular interaction with people at every stage or with varied experiences of the Christian life and prayer. They both guided people, whether formally or informally, who lived lives, in practical reality, quite different from that of fervent cloistered nuns and young friars of the reform. When their writings are read in their entirety, we see that they both give witness to the discretion and prudence that they want to find in a good spiritual director. As we read their work today, we must remember their distinctive audience.

Further, Teresa and John are explicitly seeking to assist especially those who are more mature or more advanced in the spiritual life. They felt that ample resources were available in their time for those who were new to a serious life of faith, just beginning in prayer, or just starting to walk seriously in the practice of virtue. At least some of what they say about the essential qualities of a spiritual director must be understood in this context. How important or necessary a director with learning, personal experience, and the ability to discern (and aid in discernment) is depends on the person and his or her situation at any particular moment.

There was no modern discipline of psychology when Teresa and John lived and wrote. Their principal concern was spiritual—that is, viewing one's life, relationships, and decisions in light of God's presence and action in one's life. But, at the same time, it cannot be denied that both Teresa and John were psychologically astute and full of human insight. They were gifted in their ability to understand the human situation as well as experienced in walking with others. People may have come to them or to their works with a more narrow focus on growth in prayer, but their writings make clear that they themselves had a holistic sense of the Christian life and journey. Although at first glance it may seem that the spiritual director in their minds was to be focused on the other person's life of prayer, even a superficial reading of their works makes clear that this was not the case.

Their Spiritual Vision

Consistent with the spiritual writers whom they read, Teresa and John believed that the Christian life progresses along a relatively consistent path. In traditional Catholic moral theology, we would say that they had a firm sense of the "teleological" structure of the Christian life—that is, that it is aimed at a goal ("*telos*"), *the* goal of union with God in this life or in the next (the "Beatific Vision"). They mention and were familiar with the traditional Three Ways—the idea that the Christian life generally progresses through purgative, illuminative, and unitive stages. This is not their particular lens, but they are in agreement with this idea of a dynamic progression—a relatively consistent need, with the help of God, to move from sin and vice, to grow in virtue, to progress from saying prayers to meditation to preparation for the hoped-for divine gift of contemplation. Again, because they believed that other authors addressed the initial movements through the purgative to the illuminative, they could move rather quickly to address the later movements in their own writings.

This traditional view of the Christian life as aimed at a goal is not opposed to a more relational focus. For Teresa, prayer is fundamentally about "intimate sharing" in a relationship with a God who loves us (L 8.5). Christ was ever her friend and Bridegroom. One might lose sight of the emphatically relational emphasis of John of the Cross in his prose commentaries, but in the poems themselves, the loving dialogue and relationship of the person with God is undeniable and constant. For these two authors, God invites and draws us into an ever deeper encounter and relationship—analogous to our human relationships of love—so that the final goal is not some impersonal union with an impersonal divine being but a profoundly interpersonal and infinitely dynamic union.

Today, some authors have grown uncomfortable and even suspect of this traditional view of dynamic progression along generally consistent patterns and stages. It seems to suggest some "cookie-cutter" approach to the Christian life—as if our life, prayer, and relationship with God follows "lock-step" according to a single identifiable path. That approach would seem to deny our evident and fundamental individuality and the distinctive particularities of each person's life, journey, and relationship with God. In fact, the progression through the seven dwellings of Teresa's *Interior Castle* and through the four nights of John's *Ascent of Mount Carmel* and *Dark Night* (the two are essentially two volumes of a single work) can be—and have been—read in exactly that way. But, as we shall see in the individual studies that follow, they were both aware of the inescapably distinctive nature of each person's journey. A person, after all, would not need a spiritual guide with experience and discernment if the journey were lock-step, "one-size-fits-all."

The very notion of the Christian life as a journey, a pilgrimage, or a way suggests progression toward a goal—even if the goal and growth toward it are conceived in a more explicitly relational way. And the idea of journeys and especially of pilgrimages suggests not any and all possible paths but rather certain tried and true ways, possible maps of the terrain, recognizable wrong turns and pitfalls, speedier routes, suggestions for the journey, etc. Teresa and John would have been comfortable, I suspect, with the idea of a spiritual director as an experienced and skilled guide along a journey that can include surprises and unexpected twists and turns. The director with learning, experience, and discernment is ready to assist with those variations—not to push one along some kind of idealized, one-and-only path.

A final word about spiritual vision: following a great deal of mystical literature, Teresa and John believed that God dwells at the "center" of the soul. This is a central element of Teresa's mature work, the *Interior Castle*. In this perspective, their thought is consistent with many contemporary writers on contemplative practice who believe that God, in the words of Thomas Merton, is the "Hidden Ground of Love" of each person. And these modern authors—consistent with traditional ascetical perspectives (though often with a greater role given to the contemplative practice itself)—see that we must strip away what stands between us and our resting in and drawing true life from this Hidden Ground. The danger is that this focus on God within or as a ground of our being will be seen as too interior or as individualistic. But Teresa tells us that when the person, in the seventh dwelling, attains transformative union with God, she or he discovers in a new way that the task is works of love for neighbor! As Merton writes, to draw more deeply into communion with God is to discover our deep, intrinsic connectedness with everyone else. Of that truth, Teresa and John were well aware.

With the above context in mind, we are now ready to look more particularly, first at the works of Teresa of Avila, and then at those of John of the Cross.

Part Two

Teresa of Avila

Teresa of Jesus was a person anxious to receive good direction. She consulted widely and often. Some directors, she felt, helped her very little (L 4.7; 5.3; 6.4; 8.11). Others, she felt, actually did her harm—for example, by consulting others too widely about her experience so that it became the topic of local wonderment and gossip (L 23.13). Still others harmed her by their lack of prudence and discernment in addressing her actual needs at a particular moment or because of ignorance or lack of personal experience in deeper matters of prayer (L 23.6–15). But, at the same time, she felt herself blessed to have found still other guides who proved to be of great assistance to her because of their knowledge, personal experience of prayer, and discerning spirit, as we will see below in reviewing her experiences of direction as she describes it in the *Life*.

In the process of these many and varied relationships and encounters, Teresa gained great insight into what makes for good, not-so-good, and even bad spiritual guides (recognizing, of course, that a "good" spiritual guide may not be best suited for any particular individual!). Furthermore, her experience of the spiritual companionship offered by others, her own innate gifts, together with her profound experience of God and personal journey of transformation made of her a learned, experienced, and prudent guide for others. In the chapters that follow in this second part, we will look at Teresa's personal experience of direction, the characteristics that she came to believe to be essential in any good director, her own experience as a spiritual guide for others, and her holistic view of the spiritual life as the broader subject matter of spiritual direction.

Chapter Three

Teresa of Avila, Directed

Anxious for Guidance

In an introductory chapter, we laid out some elements of the historical context that help us to understand some of the distinctive emphases on the topic of spiritual direction offered by Teresa and John of the Cross. Teresa herself reports to us her own experience of direction and particularly her eagerness to seek sound guidance. As we have seen, sixteenth-century Spain was a time of great spiritual fervor. There was a hunger for deeper prayer and for a faith that could move far beyond mere ritual and adherence to rules and customs. But it was also a time of poor catechesis and widespread illiteracy, and so, this fervor could lead to aberrations from basic tenets of the Catholic faith and practice. Many who gained widespread fame as mystics and visionaries proved to be charlatans, in league with the demonic, or perhaps more often simply misguided. The Inquisition was active throughout the century, looking explicitly for such aberrant Christianity. And the inquisitors believed that they found it notably among nuns and laywomen (who would have been less likely to be well catechized or literate and whom the prevailing culture prejudged to be less capable of the critical thought and reflection that might have kept them on a proper course).

It is in this context, especially as she began to enter into mystical experiences of prayer—ecstasies, visions, and locutions—that Teresa felt a strong need to be guided by knowledgeable people who could keep her from going astray like those widely known examples around her. Perhaps part of this was an explicit fear of finding herself under the vigilant investigative gaze of the Inquisition. Her friends warned her of this possibility. And while she says that she laughed it off, she was quite capable of seeing the danger involved. But, more fundamentally, Teresa herself was deeply committed to the truth of the faith as presented by the Scriptures and the Church—a truth from which she firmly did not want to stray. There is no reason to doubt her utter sincerity when she replied to friends who warned her about the Inquisition: "This amused me and made me laugh, for I never had any fear of such a possibility. If anyone were to see that I went against the slightest ceremony of the Church in a matter of faith, I myself knew well that I would die a thousand deaths for the faith or for any truth of Sacred Scripture" (L 33.5).

But under the surface of her writing, we see a self-critical spirit that placed a foundational importance on truth and authentic self-knowledge and therefore a profound aversion to self-deceit and illusion. When, for example, she begins the explanation of the inner, spiritual journey described in the *Interior*

Castle, she tells us that it can be begun only with prayer and self-knowledge (IC 1.1.7 and 1.2.8–9). When she sets out to explain prayer in its successive deepening in the *Way of Perfection*, she tells her readers that an essential foundation is humility, which she defines as "to walk in truth" (W 4.4; see also L 22.11).

For Teresa, the need for such self-knowledge is not a single step in that path; it is necessary in every season of the spiritual life. She tells us in the *Life*:

> This path of self-knowledge must never be abandoned, nor is there on this journey a soul so much a giant that it has no need to return often to the stage of an infant and a suckling. And this should never be forgotten. Perhaps I shall speak of it more often because it is very important. There is no stage of prayer so sublime that it isn't necessary to return often to the beginning. Along this path of prayer, self-knowledge and the thought of one's sins is the bread with which all palates must be fed no matter how delicate they may be; they cannot be sustained without this bread. (L 13.15)

She makes the same point in the *Interior Castle*: "Knowing ourselves is something so important that I wouldn't want any relaxation ever in this regard, however high you may have climbed into the heavens. While we are on this earth nothing is more important to us than humility" (IC 1.2.9). Even in the *Foundations*—while offering a narrative of the monasteries that she founded—this great mystic and teacher of prayer tells us: "I consider one day of humble self-knowledge a greater favor from the Lord, even though the day may have cost us numerous afflictions and trials, than many days of prayer" (F 5.16).

Teresa of Jesus was personally and profoundly committed to the path of self-knowledge and walking in truth, and she believed that she needed the right spiritual guides to assist her in this task—companions learned in the faith to prevent her from going off course, experienced in prayer in order to help identify pitfalls and false directions, and discerning of the movements both of the Holy Spirit and of the individual human hearts of flesh-and-blood people.

But spiritual directors can provide such assistance in the person's maintenance and growth in self-knowledge only if he or she is completely honest and forthright: "What is necessary, Sisters, is that you proceed very openly and truthfully with your confessor. I don't mean in regard to telling your sins, for that is obvious, but in giving an account of your prayer. If you do not give such an account, I am not sure you are proceeding well, nor that it is God who is teaching you" (IC 6.9.12). And in the *Life* (26.3) she says of herself: "The safest thing, as the Lord told me, is to make known to my confessor the whole state of my soul and the favors God grants me, that he be learned, and that I obey him. The Lord has often told me this. It is what I do, and without doing so I would have no peace." On the other hand, Teresa herself also manifests the unfortunate results of failing to do so. She reports in the *Life* that she was not honest and self-revealing with one of her very first directors, Gaspar Daza (as we shall see in more detail below). While it is true that he was not discerning in that he tried to push her beyond her current state of readiness, it is also true that Teresa reports that she was too embarrassed by her self-perceived failings and his apparent high opinion of her to make an honest confession of her state (L 23.8).

Directors and Confessors

In the writings of Teresa of Jesus, the most common term for what we today would call a spiritual director is "confessor." In fact, she says of herself that she was fond of the sacrament (L 5.9), and she was concerned that her nuns would be able to participate in the sacrament with competent confessors. Of course, she understood clearly the distinction between the sacrament of penance and spiritual direction, but in fact she often received her direction within the sacrament, at the time that she met for the sacrament (though perhaps separate from it), and from priests who were her regular confessors for a time.

Today, spiritual directors who are priests are widely, rightly, and prudently cautioned to distinguish the sacrament from spiritual direction—not trying to offer wider spiritual guidance in the context of the sacrament. This is especially true when the sacramental reconciliation is being offered in a parish on a typical Saturday afternoon or before Sunday Masses while other penitents wait. Sound spiritual accompaniment is broader and deeper in its scope than the discussion of sins and vices, requiring a more consistent and stable relationship than a typical parish confessional practice can permit. And yet, at the same time, sin—especially habitual, chronic, or serious sin—most usually has much deeper and wider roots and entanglements in our lives and relationships with God and others than can be enumerated or described in the sacrament. Teresa of Jesus was most definitely concerned to speak far more broadly and deeply with many of her confessors than a simple enumeration of sin—but obstacles to spiritual growth and the deepening of prayer were one of her deep concerns.

Directors, Good and Bad, in the Life

In the *Book of Her Life*, Teresa identifies many of her confessors, especially for the critical period between 1554, when she had her "conversion" and the beginning of her mystical experiences, and 1562, when the narration of the *Life* ends.[1] Her *Spiritual Testimony* 58 (1576), probably written as a statement for the Inquisition, lists many of the respected and learned theologians from whom she received guidance over the years. These included the Jesuits Diego de Cetina, Baltasar Alvárez, Francis Borgia, Gaspar de Salazar, Juan de Prádanos, and Pedro Doménech; the Dominicans Vicente Barrón, Pedro Ibáñez, Domingo Báñez, and García de Toledo; and the Franciscan Pedro de Alcántara. In addition, in the *Life*, the reader is introduced to the spiritual friends who offered her additional support, guidance, and recommendations: the "saintly gentleman" (L 23.6) Francisco de Salcedo, the diocesan priest Gaspar Daza, the Augustinian nun María de Briceño (L 3.1), and Teresa's uncle Don Pedro Sánchez de Cepeda (L 3.4) as well as her friends and supporters, Doña Guillomar de Ulloa and Doña Luisa de la Cerda. It was these relationships and encounters that helped Teresa form her view of effective spiritual direction.

1. In this section, I am drawing especially from the helpful examination of these confessors offered by María Trinidad González González, "Dirección espiritual y transformación interior en Santa Teresa de Jesús" (STL thesis, Universidad Pontificia Comillas de Madrid, Instituto de Teología Espiritual, 2006), 9–23. For a brief biography of each director, consult the biographical section of Tomás Álvarez, ed., *Diccionario de Santa Teresa*, 2nd ed. (Burgos, Spain: Editorial Monte Carmelo, 2006).

We will not attempt to identify and narrate at length the spiritual guidance offered by all of Teresa's directors. That would easily be a book-length discussion in itself. But a brief summary of her first real experiences as a directee, as she describes in the *Life*, will serve as a good introduction to the examination of the characteristics that she believed should be possessed by a good director. (Teresa mentions the names of a number of other, later directors in her letters. See also ST 58.)

One of Teresa's first confessors of spiritual depth was the Dominican theologian Vicente Barrón, who was her father's confessor in the final period of his life before his death in 1544 (L 7.16–17). At the time, already a nun, Teresa had given up the consistent practice of quiet prayer, and Barrón offered her encouragement and support in returning to it. In the years ahead, they would cross paths sporadically, and she would take the opportunity to seek his counsel. Teresa does not explicitly mention another confessor for the ten-year period between 1544 and 1554, and it is possible that Barrón continued in that capacity during some of that time.

In Lent of 1554, Teresa had a profound spiritual experience through a chance encounter with an image of the wounded Christ and a reading of the *Confessions* of Saint Augustine. This opened up a new depth of prayer and ultimately extraordinary spiritual experiences that made her realize the necessity of finding a "spiritual person" (L 23.3) to guide her. At the recommendation of the "saintly gentleman" Francisco Salcedo, she went for a time to a highly respected and learned diocesan priest of Avila, Gaspar Daza. But he failed to understand her experience, pressed her impatiently in directions for which she felt unprepared, and ultimately judged her experiences to be demonic (L 23.6–15)—much to her dismay. In this early experience, Teresa must have begun to form her sense that a director must be learned, but, more than learned, also attentive to the individual as well as experienced in the spiritual life.

Providentially in Teresa's view, friends recommended that she consult the Jesuits who had only recently arrived in Avila (and were, in fact, only of recent origin).[2] They had a reputation for being men of deep prayer and experience. The recently ordained Diego de Cetina became her confessor for a few months between 1554 and 1555, and, with him, she felt understood, consoled, and renewed (L 23.16–18). It was around this time, in 1557, that Teresa was able to meet the future St. Francis Borgia, SJ, who was passing through the area. Formerly the Duke of Gandía and close confidant of Spanish royalty, he had left that life behind, become a Jesuit, and developed a reputation for holiness (and was later canonized). Teresa and Francis met only twice, but the conversations were intense and left her greatly consoled (L 24.3; ST 58.3).

The transfer of the young Cetina after only a short time had left Teresa deeply concerned for the progress of her spiritual life, but her friend Guiomar de Ulloa, herself a woman

2. See Terence O'Reilly, "St. Teresa and Her First Jesuit Confessors," in *St. Teresa of Ávila: Her Writings and Life*, ed. Terence O'Reilly, Colin P. Thompson, and Lesley Twomey, Studies in Hispanic and Lusophone Cultures 19 (Cambridge, England: Legenda [Modern Humanities Research Association], 2018), 108–23. He focuses particular attention on Diego de Cetina and Juan de Prádanos, 115–21.

of great prayer, brought her into contact with her own confessor, another young Jesuit, Juan de Prádanos (L 24.4–8) who served as Teresa's director during the years 1555 to 1558. He encouraged her and even gently challenged her, especially in the matter of personal attachments that he perceived were an obstacle. But he did so in a prudent way, ultimately urging her to take the matter to prayer, offering it to God while praying the *Veni, Creator Spiritus* ("Come, Creator Spirit"). In that prayer, she entered into a rapture and heard God say to her: "No longer do I want you to converse with men but with angels." More deeply, she felt freed of her excessive attachments to persons, and she credits her confessor with recognizing the obstacle but also knowing when to push and when to leave the matter to the Holy Spirit (L 24.7). This experience contrasts with that described in the previous chapter of the *Life* in which the learned and sincere Gaspar Daza had pushed her too hard in the direction that he himself thought best.

With the departure of Juan de Prádanos, Teresa turned to yet another young, recently ordained Jesuit, Baltasar Álvarez. He accompanied her through much of the period of her intense mystical experiences—visions, ecstasies, and raptures—between 1559 and 1565 (ST 58.3). Her description of him in the *Life* (28.14–17) anticipates much about her personal experience of what she later described as essential in good spiritual direction. She reveals him as discreet and prudent, even as she describes herself as an indiscreet directee who shared her experiences too widely. It may be helpful to quote her description at length, highlighting several words and phrases, and then offer further comment:

Insofar as I know, my confessor, as I say—who was a truly holy Father from the Society of Jesus—gave this same reply. He was *very discreet and deeply humble*; and this humility that was so great brought upon me many trials. For since *he was a learned and very prayerful man, and the Lord didn't lead him by this path*, he didn't trust in himself. He suffered many great trials in many ways on my account. I knew that they told him to be careful of me, that he shouldn't let the devil deceive him by anything I told him; they brought up examples to him of other persons. All of this made me anxious. I feared that I would have no one who would hear my confession, but that all would run from me. I did nothing but weep.

By God's providence he wanted to continue to hear my confession, for he was such a great servant of God that he would have put up with anything for God; so he advised me that I shouldn't turn aside from what he told me or fear that he would fail me, and that I shouldn't offend God. *He always encouraged and comforted me. He always ordered me not to hold anything from him. I never did.* He told me that if I followed this advice the devil wouldn't be able to harm me even if the vision did come from him, but that rather the Lord would draw good out of the evil the devil desired to do my soul. This Father *strove for my soul's perfection in every way he could.* Since I had so much fear, I obeyed him in everything, although imperfectly; for on account of these trials he suffered a great deal during the three years or more that he was my confessor.[3] In the great persecutions I suffered and in the many bad judgments the Lord allowed others to make of me—and often

---

3. Elsewhere (ST 58.3), as we have seen, she says that he directed her for six years. It may be that she is thinking of three particularly trying years.

without their being at fault—everyone came to him, and he was blamed without any fault on his part.

It would have been impossible for him to suffer so much if he hadn't been so holy and the Lord hadn't encouraged him. He had to respond to those who thought I was going astray; and they didn't believe him. On the other hand *he had to calm me and heal the fear I had* by putting greater stress on the fear of offending God. *He also had to assure me*, for since in each vision there was something new, God permitted that I afterward be left with great fears. Everything happened to me because I was and had been such a sinner. *This Father comforted me with great pity. If he would have trusted in himself more, I wouldn't have suffered so much; God gave him understanding of the truth in all things—the very Sacrament itself enlightened him, I believe.*

Those servants of God who were not so sure about me conversed with me often. *Since I spoke carelessly about some things,* they interpreted my intention differently and thought that what I said, without my being careful, as I say, showed little humility. (I loved one of them very much because my soul owed him an infinite debt and he was very holy; I felt it infinitely when I saw that he didn't understand me; he strongly desired that I might advance and that the Lord might give me light). Upon seeing some little fault in me—for they saw many—everything else was immediately condemned. They asked me some things; I answered plainly and carelessly. At once they supposed that I wanted to teach them and that I thought I was wise. It would all get back to my confessor, for certainly they desired my good; and he would again scold me. [Emphasis added throughout.]

Teresa describes Álvarez as a person of learning and prayer but not himself called to the mystical path—that is, he was not "experienced" in the specific path to which she was called. Nonetheless, his own prayerful humility about a path that he did not personally walk and especially his openness to the working of the Spirit in this ministry allowed God to give him the necessary understanding to be of real assistance to her. In fact, had he been more self-confident and more trusting in his discernment of the movement of the Spirit (he was probably only twenty-five or so when he began as her director), Teresa feels that he might have been of even more help to her in her journey in that period.

Further, it is apparent that Álvarez was attentive to her fear and the barrage of criticism she faced. He was therefore comforting and encouraging, though not afraid to push and challenge Teresa. Perhaps their mutual reference to obedience in this context is a sign of the religious culture of the time, though it appears just as clear that Álvarez had discerned that Teresa's fear—together with the bad advice that she was receiving elsewhere—made a more directive approach more apt for her during that time. At the same time, his insistence on honest self-revelation—and her commitment to it—surely made their relationship more fruitful. In his loyalty to their relationship, despite the personal cost to himself, he reveals a firm commitment to their spiritual friendship even when Teresa herself doubted that anyone else would have remained with her.

During this same period in which she was being directed by Álvarez, Teresa met the Franciscan, already renowned for his holiness (and later a saint), Pedro de Alcántara—again through her spiritual friend Guiomar de Ulloa and in her home. Their conversations were brief but intense and apparently reciprocally fruitful—focused both on her thoughts of initiating the reform and her experiences of and her questions about prayer (L 30.2–7). She says that she was especially helped because he understood her immediately because he himself had experience (L 30.4).

The Dominican Pedro Ibáñez, a professor at the Dominican friary of Santo Tomas in Avila, assisted and advised Teresa in the foundation of her first monastery of the reform, Saint Joseph (L 32.16–18). But he subsequently became a confessor and director (L 33.5–6; ST 58.8), which became a source for his own deep spiritual growth (L 33.6).

As the new foundation was beginning to take shape, a new Jesuit superior arrived in Avila, Gaspar de Salazar, and Teresa found in him a new spiritual guide. She found him to be a man of learning, pure and holy, and possessing a special gift for discerning spirits (L 33.7–10). He too was able to give her counsel about both the foundation and her life of prayer.

In 1562, Teresa—following a typical practice of the time—was sent to Toledo to serve as a comfort for a recently widowed noblewoman, Luisa de la Cerda. And it was through her that Teresa met (or perhaps became reacquainted with) the Dominican García de Toledo (L 34.6–8), and they discovered a deep spiritual affinity for one another. It was he who instructed her to write down her experiences of prayer in what became the *Book of Her Life* (L 10.7–8). Again, his guidance of Teresa—and her special prayer for him—brought him great benefit (L 34.6–17). We see in him, once again, a man of learning and discernment. And while ultimately he would himself grow in a more profound prayer, Teresa notes that what he didn't know from his own experience, his humility and learning allowed him to study so that he could offer fruitful counsel to her (L 34.13). She offers a general comment about situations such as these: "I don't say that anyone who has not had spiritual experience, provided he is a learned man, should not guide someone who has. But he ought to limit himself to seeing to it that in both exterior and interior matters the soul walks in conformity to the natural way through the use of reason; and in supernatural experiences he should see that it walks in conformity with Sacred Scripture. As for the rest he shouldn't kill himself or think he understands what he doesn't, or suppress the spirit; for now, in respect to the spirit, another greater Lord governs them; they are not without a Superior" (L 34.11). Teresa and García de Toledo maintained a strong and friendly relationship with mutual respect and affection (L 16.6; 40.23–24).

Although it takes us slightly beyond the period narrated in the *Life*, we note that one of her later directors/confessors was the young John of the Cross. They had met in 1567 when John was twenty-five years old and very recently ordained and when Teresa was fifty-two, already advanced in prayer and founder of the reform. She had convinced him not to leave the Carmelite Order for the more contemplative Carthusians but rather become part of her soon-to-be initiated male branch of the reform (F 3.17). We do not know anything about the spiritual progress of the young friar at that moment, but he undoubtedly learned a great deal from her in the early days of the establishment of the reform. But in 1572, after Teresa had been ordered to return to the Monastery of the

Incarnation as prioress, she arranged to have John appointed as confessor. He subsequently became her own confessor and director for those few years that they coincided there. And it was during this time that Teresa entered the "spiritual marriage"—that is, the transformative union with God in November 1572 (ST 31).

The *Life* is a treasure house of narrated experience that Teresa had during her early years as a person of deep prayer and a reformer. Although she left no such narration about later directors, the *Life* gives us a clear view of the foundations from which she derived her conclusion that a reliable spiritual guide must be learned, experienced, and discerning. And to those characteristics—as they are discussed in the works of Teresa of Jesus—we now turn.

Chapter Four

The Three Essential Characteristics

All Three of Them

Amid the spiritual fervor of sixteenth-century Spain, the Franciscans in particular developed and encouraged a life of prayer deeper than external rituals and established prayers and devotions. It was from their tradition that Teresa learned the "prayer of recollection": the drawing in or gathering of the senses and conscious attention into quiet, wordless prayer, first by our own graced effort and then hopefully by the gifted work of God. But the Franciscans went further by encouraging such prayer among ordinary people—laywomen and laymen as well as religious and priests. This development was opposed by many academically educated clergy (and later by the Inquisition) as dangerous in a time of poor catechesis and illiteracy, especially among women (including nuns). Conflict arose among those "with learning" (*letrados*) and those "with experience" (*espirituales*). Those with academic degrees warned of the dangers of heresy arising among those misguided by their felt experiences of God, while those who had enjoyed a depth of prayer argued that dry academic learning could offer very little to the actual mature spiritual life of the faithful. But both Teresa and John bridged this divide by insisting on the necessity of both learning and actual spiritual experience in those who would guide others—education and experience joined with a spiritual prudence and discernment in assisting others on the Christian path.

Teresa offers one her earliest and lengthiest reflections on these three qualities—learning, experience, and discernment—in the *Life*. Below we quote her teaching at length since it reveals directly the importance of each of them as well as the three of them together; ideally, all three characteristics would be present together in a spiritual guide. Note that she indicates a certain order of their importance, but she says that she herself has gotten it jumbled. In the end, perhaps she might say that the relative importance of any of the characteristics—recognizing the importance of all—depends on the individual and his or her actual situation at a particular moment.

Beginners need counsel so as to see what helps them most. For this reason a master is very necessary providing he has experience. If he doesn't, he can be greatly mistaken and lead a soul without understanding it nor allowing it to understand itself. For since it sees that there is great merit in being subject to a master, it doesn't dare depart from what he commands it. I have come upon souls intimidated and afflicted for whom I felt great pity because the one who taught them had no experience; and there was one person who didn't know what to do with herself. Since they do not understand spiritual things, these masters afflict soul and body and obstruct progress. One of these souls spoke to me about a master who held her bound for eight years and wouldn't let her go beyond self-knowledge; the Lord had already brought her to the prayer of quiet, and so she suffered much tribulation. . . .

So it is very important that the master have prudence—I mean that he have good judgment—and experience; if besides these he has learning, so much the better. But if one cannot find these three qualifications together, the first two are more important since men with a background in studies can be sought out and consulted when there is need. I say that if these learned men do not practice prayer their learning is of little help to beginners. I do not mean that beginners shouldn't consult learned men, for I would rather a spirit without prayer than one that has not begun to walk in truth. Also, learning is a great thing because learned men teach and enlighten us who know little; and, when brought before the truths of Sacred Scripture, we do what we ought. May God deliver us from foolish devotions.

I want to explain myself further, for I believe I'm getting mixed up in many things. I've always had this fault of not knowing how to explain myself, as I have said, except at the cost of many words. A nun begins to practice prayer. If a foolish and whimsical person is directing her, he will explain that it is better for her to obey him than her superior. He does this without malice but thinks he is doing right, because if he is not a religious, such advice will seem to be good. And when dealing with matters in the home if the person is a married woman, he will tell her that it is better to remain in prayer if it displeases her husband. Thus he doesn't know how to arrange time or things so that they be conformed to truth. Since he lacks the light himself, he doesn't know how to enlighten others even though he may want to do so. And although it seems that learning is not necessary for such knowledge, my opinion has always been and will be that every Christian strive to speak if possible with someone who has gone through studies; and the more learned the person the better. Those who walk the path of prayer have a greater need for this counsel; and the more spiritual they are, the greater their need.

Let not the spiritual person be misled by saying that learned men without prayer are unsuitable for those who practice it. I have consulted many learned men because for some years now, on account of a greater necessity, I have sought them out more; and I've always been a friend of men of learning. For though some don't have experience, they don't despise the Spirit nor do they ignore it, because in Sacred Scripture, which they study, they always find the truth of the good spirit. I hold that the devil will not deceive with illusions the person of prayer who consults learned men, unless this person wants to be deceived, because the devils have a tremendous fear of that learning which is accompanied by humility and virtue; and they know they will be discovered and go away with a loss.

I have said this because there are opinions going around that learned men if they are not spiritual are of no help to people who practice prayer. I have already said that it is necessary to have a spiritual master; but if he is not a learned man, this lack of learning will be a hindrance. It will be a great help to consult with learned men. If they are virtuous even though they may not experience spiritual things, they will benefit me; and God will enable them to explain what they must teach— He will even give them spiritual experience so that they might help us. I do not say this without having experienced it, and it has happened to me with more than two. I say that if individuals are going to submit completely to only one master, they would be greatly mistaken if they did not seek one like this since if he is a religious he must be subject to his superior. For perhaps the master will be lacking all the three qualities of a good master, which will be no small cross, especially if the soul is unwilling to submit to one with poor judgment. At least I haven't been able to submit in this way myself; nor do I think such submission is fitting. But those who belong to the laity, let them praise God that they can choose someone to whom they may be subject and not lose this very virtuous freedom. Let them, however, postpone having a master until a suitable person is found, for the Lord will provide one on the condition that all is founded upon humility and the desire to do the right thing. I praise God greatly, and women and those who haven't gone through studies must always be infinitely grateful to Him that there be someone who by means of so many labors has attained that truth which ignorant people don't know. (L 13.14, 16–19)

Describing some of the extraordinary mystical experiences that characterize the sixth dwelling places of the *Interior Castle*, Teresa speaks explicitly of the need for learning and experience in a director—and implicitly about discretion.

It is good that at the beginning you speak about this vision under the seal of confession with a very learned man, for learned men will give us light. Or, with some very spiritual person, if there be one available; if there isn't, it's better to speak with a very learned man. Or with both a spiritual person and a learned man if both are at hand. And should they tell you the vision is fancied, do not be concerned, for the fancy can do little good or evil. Commend yourself to the divine Majesty that he not let you be deceived. If they should tell you your vision is from the devil, it will be a greater trial, although no one will say this if he is indeed learned and the effects mentioned are present. But if he says so, I know that the Lord Himself who walks with you will console you, assure you, and give the confessor light that he may give it to you.

If the confessor is a person whom, although he practices prayer, the Lord has not led by this path, he will at once be frightened and condemn it. For this reason I advise you to have a confessor who is very learned and, if possible, also spiritual. The prioress should give permission for such consultation. Even though, judging by the good life you live, you may be walking securely, the prioress will be obligated to have you speak with a confessor so that both you and she may walk securely. And once you have spoken with these persons, be quiet and don't try to confer about the matter with others; at times the devil causes some fears so excessive that they force the soul, without its having anything really to fear, not to be satisfied with one consultation. If, especially, the confessor has little experience, and the soul sees that he is fearful, and he himself makes it continue to speak of the matter, that which by rights should have remained very secret is made public, and this soul is persecuted and tormented. (IC 6.8.8–9)

Clearly, for Teresa, all three characteristics are important in a truly good spiritual guide. Keeping the above texts in mind, let us look closely at each of three qualities.

The Director as Learned

Teresa of Jesus lived in a religious culture that was very concerned about the activity of the devil and the ways that the evil one can deceive us, even about experiences and promptings that seem to be of God. As we saw in an earlier chapter, sixteenth-century Spain was a period of greater spiritual fervor but also of misguided and false mystics. And, with added concern about heresy and the influx of Protestant ideas, the Inquisition was actively pursuing the possibility of such mystical aberrations, especially among women. In such a context, Teresa was prudent enough frequently to seek out sound theological advice about her experience and critical review of her writings. With that background in mind, we can see that "learned" for Teresa meant someone academically trained in theology and biblical studies who could caution her about any potential errors in the personal interpretation of her experience and in her written expression of it. Most of Teresa's confessors and guides were priests with just such academic preparation. She says of herself: "I've always been a friend of men of learning" (L 13.8).

Of particular importance to Teresa was that her experience—and her understanding of it—be in accord with what has been revealed in the Sacred Scriptures. She reports, for example, that she benefited from a bishop with whom she consulted in the course of her foundations: "But, in fact, he was very helpful to me because he assured me with passages from Sacred Scripture, which is what suits me most when I am sure that one knows it well. I knew he did and that he lived a good life" (F 30.1).

On the other hand, Teresa reports that she was harmed by "half-learned" guides who misinterpreted her experience and gave her unhelpful counsel because of their lack of learning: "I have had a great deal of experience with learned men, and have also had experience with half-learned, fearful ones; these latter cost me dearly" (IC 5.1.8). She says elsewhere: "It happened to me that I spoke about matters of conscience with a confessor who had gone through the whole course of theology, and he did me a great deal of harm by telling me that some matters didn't amount to anything. I know that he didn't intend to misinform me and had no reason to, but he simply didn't know any more. And the same thing happened to me with two or three others, besides the one I mentioned" (W 5.3);[1] it is not clear precisely to whom this last comment refers.

Early in the *Life*, as she was narrating the crippling illness that afflicted her as a young nun, she says:

> There was a cleric of excellent intelligence and social status who lived in that place where I went to be cured. He was learned, although not greatly so. I began to confess to him, for I was always fond of learning. Half-learned confessors have done my soul great harm when I have been unable to find a confessor with as much learning as I like. I have come to see by experience that it is better, if they are virtuous and observant of holy customs, that they have little learning. For then they do not trust themselves without asking someone

1. The title of this fifth chapter of the *Way of Perfection* is "Continues on the subject of confessors. Speaks of the importance of their being learned."

who knows, nor do I trust them; and a truly learned man had never misguided me. Those others certainly could not have wanted to mislead me, but they didn't know any better. (L 5.3)

But Teresa's desire for regular counsel from learned people was not simply a concern about drifting into heresy and arousing the attention of the Inquisition. As we have seen, she was innately and passionately a person seeking the truth about God and about herself. She feared and detested the idea of being self-deceived and becoming blinded by illusion. She says of herself: "I have always tried to find someone who would give me light" (L 10.8). Humility is a central element of her spiritual teaching, and she defines it as "walking in truth." If we hope to grow in the spiritual life, we must walk in the truth of who God is and who we are before God.

It is true that Teresa's concern for finding a truly learned director must be understood in the context of her historical culture and her distinctive perspective. Widespread illiteracy and poor basic catechesis, together with the fear and reality of heresy and misguided mystics as well as demonic influence, would have undoubtedly heightened the need for a director with formal academic theological and biblical training. Moreover, Teresa was experiencing extraordinary mystical phenomena, calling for careful guidance in order to be kept from being led off-course by a mistaken personal interpretation of her experience. And Teresa herself was guiding fervent Discalced nuns and their clerical and lay friends who were pursuing deep contemplative prayer and perhaps experiencing extraordinary phenomena such as visions.

We are not living in sixteenth-century Spain. Probably few of us have experienced the kinds of extraordinary experiences Teresa describes (though I have spoken to many people who believe that—or at least wonder if—they have been blessed, from time to time, by some special communication from God). Perhaps many of us are not yet at a point in our own spiritual journey that we feel ready or even called to seek deep contemplative prayer (though I suspect that Teresa would urge us to do so). And so, we do not need learned guides in the exact sense that Teresa desired. And yet, self-deception is as much a danger for us as it was in Teresa's time. We too must be committed to "walking in truth" through a critical self-knowledge. We live today in an age of subjectivism in which we may be tempted to place too much trust in our own personal experience, interpretations, and opinions over claims of objective truth as these are revealed by Scripture and tradition. There is the potential danger in the realm of contemplative literature today to pass into understandings of God that seem more in line with Eastern religions and New Age religions than sound Christian doctrine. If we are Christians, we continue to believe, as Teresa did, that the Scriptures are the inspired Word of God and a sure guide for our lives. If we are Catholic, we believe that the Church has reliable doctrine to keep us on a sound course in our thinking, reflection on our experience, and discernment. Perhaps today, many people do not need a guide with formal academic biblical and theological training—though, prudently, it seems to me, contemporary certificate and other training programs in spiritual accompaniment do include learning about key biblical and theological themes as well as the history of Christian spirituality. It may be true that many of us do not need guides with academic degrees in theology. But perhaps as we advance in our spiritual journey and prayer, such training in a director might become particularly important.

Experienced/Spiritual

For Teresa, a spiritual guide must have spiritual experience. In this, she is not so much speaking of practical experience in the guidance of others. In fact, many of her early Jesuit directors/confessors were quite young and only recently ordained. One would presume, at the same time, that actual experience as a director would make one more attentive, more discerning, and more able to offer probing questions and comment based on previous relationships of companioning others. This is not so different from the way that counselors, physicians, and teachers become better at their craft by practice.

But Teresa's concern is really experience in prayer and in the ways of the Spirit. As much as she values a director with learning, she knows that the director is not simply a teacher of spiritual doctrine who directs persons along a one-size-fits-all path. The guidance of another along the journey of the Christian life requires in the guide such things as actual personal experience of the ways and the movements of the Spirit, personal knowledge of the difficulties and possible pitfalls of the journey, and personal encounter with God. The ideal in a director, she says, is not learning or experience but both.

At the same time, we must remember that Teresa was writing especially for those who desired and were actively pursuing prayer well beyond what we might call its beginnings. She felt that there was abundant literature available to assist those setting out on the journey of prayer and of the Christian life more broadly. More, she herself began earnestly to seek direction when her prayer deepened to the point that she began to experience extraordinary phenomena. When Teresa speaks of direction, then, she is most often thinking of spiritual guides for contemplatives (whether by personal vocation or by state in life) and those of deep prayer and even with mystical experiences. And so, when she is speaking of the spiritual experience necessary to guide others, she is often referring to the necessity—or at least to the desirability or optimality—of directors who themselves have begun to experience such deep prayer as well as the potential pitfalls that can arise along the way. This fact does not eliminate the value of her comments on experience more broadly—surely we want spiritual guides today who have an active personal relationship with God and familiarity with the ways of prayer—but it is helpful to remember her particular emphasis.

Lack of deep experience in the director can lead to serious problems, as Teresa counsels:

> Let us begin with the torment one meets with from a confessor who is so discreet and has so little experience [*tan cuerdo y poco experimentado*] that there is nothing he is sure of: he fears everything and finds in everything something to doubt because he sees these unusual experiences. He becomes especially doubtful if he notices some imperfection in a soul that has them, for it seems to such confessors that the ones to whom God grants these favors must be angels—but that is impossible as long as they are in this body. Everything is immediately condemned as from the devil or melancholy. (IC 6.1.8)

Speaking particularly about the experience of raptures or ecstasies in prayer, Teresa says: "If those who guide them have not gone through this themselves, it may perhaps seem to these guides, especially if they aren't learned men, that these persons are as though dead during the rapture. And, as I shall say afterward, what these persons suffer when their confessors do not understand them is a pity" (L 20.21).

Again, speaking particularly about those who have had mystical experiences in the sixth dwelling places, Teresa says: "If the confessor is a person whom, although he practices prayer, the Lord has not led by this path, he will at once be frightened and condemn it. For this reason I advise you to have a confessor who is very learned and, if possible, also spiritual" (IC 6.8.9). This is what she, in fact, experienced early in her deepening prayer when a director told her that her experiences were of demonic origin, instructing her to make an obscene gesture at any vision of Christ that she experienced (L 29.5–6). This caused her much distress, and she tells us elsewhere that a man with learning was able to assure her that she had received bad counsel in the matter (IC 6.9.13).

In the *Life*, she recounts how Peter of Alcántara was able to help her precisely because of his experience:

Almost from the outset I saw that he understood me through experience, which was all that I needed. For at that time I didn't understand myself or how to describe my experiences as I do now (for afterward God enabled me to understand and describe the favors that His Majesty granted me), and it was necessary that the one who understood me and explained these experiences to me should himself have experienced them. Friar Peter greatly enlightened me; I couldn't understand that such an experience was possible, at least as regards the visions that were not imaginative. It seemed to me that I didn't understand either how those I saw with the eyes of my soul were possible. As I have said, only those that were seen with the bodily eyes seemed to me to merit attention, and I didn't experience these.

This holy man enlightened me about everything and explained it to me, and he told me not to be grieved but that I should praise God and be so certain that all was from His Spirit that with the exception of the faith nothing could for me be truer or more believable. He was much consoled along with me and showed me every kind regard and favor, and ever afterward he was very solicitous for me and shared with me his own concerns and business matters. Since he saw that I had desires for what he possessed in deed—for the Lord gave me these in a very definite way—and saw that I had so much courage, he was glad to talk to me. For anyone the Lord brings to this state finds no pleasure or consolation equal to that of meeting someone to whom they think the Lord has begun to grant these desires. I couldn't then have had many more, in my opinion, and please God I may have them now.

He took the greatest pity on me. He told me that one of the worst trials on earth was the one I had suffered (which is contradiction on the part of good men), and that I had still a long way to go; for I was always in need and there was no one in this city who understood me. But he said that he would speak to my confessor and to the one who troubled me the most, for that was this married gentleman whom I've already mentioned. As the one who felt the greatest good-will toward me, this gentleman waged the whole opposition. He is a God-fearing and holy man; but since he had seen that I had so recently been so wretched, he wasn't able to feel assured. Thus the holy Friar Peter assured them, for he spoke to both of them and gave them motives and reasons for feeling safe and not disturbing me any more. My confessor had need of little assurance; the gentleman needed so much that the reasons were still not entirely enough, but they helped to keep him from frightening me so much. (L 30.4–6)

If the guide lacks experience as profound as the one seeking guidance, he or she should recognize that limitation and not presume to offer guidance beyond their knowledge or experience. As Teresa says in a section of the *Life* already quoted in the previous chapter:

I don't say that anyone who has not had spiritual experience, provided he is a learned man, should not guide someone who has. But he ought to limit himself to seeing to it that in both exterior and interior matters the soul walks in conformity to the natural way through the use of reason; and in supernatural experiences he should see that it walks in conformity with Sacred Scripture. As for the rest he shouldn't kill himself or think he understands what he doesn't, or suppress the spirit; for now, in respect to the spirit, another greater Lord governs them; they are not without a Superior. (L 34.11)

Again, we must acknowledge that Teresa's special concern was for the spiritual guides of those of practiced and advanced prayer. But sincere persons in every age want spiritual companions who are people of active faith, with personal knowledge of prayer's difficulties and real personal encounter with

God. Contemporary literature on the path to deeper, contemplative prayer—notably, for example, works on centering prayer (arguably the contemporary parallel of Teresa's prayer of acquired recollection)—are most often authored by avowed practitioners. At its best, such literature offers some theological and historical foundations but focuses on actual practice, often counseling regular guidance by an experienced practitioner.

Discerning/Prudent

The third recommended characteristic for a good spiritual guide according to Teresa can be broadly described by a number of English words/terms: prudent, possessing good judgment, discreet, and discerning. When Teresa lists all three qualities in the *Life* (L 13.16), she introduces this third one by calling for a prudent guide with good judgment (*maestro avisado—digo de buen entendimiento*). She goes on to give an example of the contrary—a "foolish and whimsical" guide who, though sincere and well-intentioned, lacks the prudence to give counsel in keeping with the person's actual situation and place in his or her spiritual journey (L 13.17, quoted at length at the beginning of this chapter). It is interesting to note here that, although her main point is to emphasize prudence, she continues immediately by connecting discretion with learning: "And although it seems that learning is not necessary for such knowledge, my opinion has always been and will be that every Christian strive to speak if possible with someone who has gone through studies; and the more learned the person the better."

Teresa frequently uses the term *avisado*—translated as "prudent" (e.g., L 34.7; 23.16; IC 6.3.11). But she also uses the term *discreto* (e.g., F 8.5; L 28.14) or the noun *discreción* (e.g., F 3.5, describing her director Domingo Báñez). But her concept in this regard also includes what we would call discernment of spirits, which, in one place, she refers to as *don particular del Señor para conocer espíritus* (L 33.10).

The virtue of prudence, in the Thomistic tradition, is the acquired, abiding ability or disposition to decide well. It includes the ability to be discerning in the sense of being able to size up a situation and the people involved as well as bring together a wider body of knowledge and experience as they may be applicable in a particular situation. In its simple, human form, discretion is the abiding ability to know how to act or to speak (or refrain from doing so) in a manner appropriate at the moment. We see the lack of human prudence in one of Teresa's early experiences of direction:

> In this respect I am speaking as one who is suffering a bitter trial because some persons with whom I have discussed my prayer are not keeping it secret, but in consulting this one and that other, they have truly done me great harm. They have spread things that should have remained very secret—these matters are not for everybody—and it seemed that I was the one who published them abroad. I believe the Lord permitted it without any fault on their part so that I might suffer. I'm not saying they spoke about what I discussed with them in confession. But since they were persons to whom because of my fears I gave an account of myself that they might enlighten me, it seemed to me they should have kept quiet. Nonetheless, I never dared to conceal anything from these persons. (L 23.13)

But prudence in the Thomistic tradition also has a supernatural form, "infused" or given by God, by which we can assess spiritual things as they direct us to God. And this infused prudence is further enhanced and perfected by the gift of counsel given by the Holy Spirit in grace. (The point here is not to argue, of course, that Teresa was trained or attempting to lay out Thomistic principles—though she had many important Dominican guides—but rather to provide a tool from the tradition to try to clarify Teresa's broad understanding of prudence or discretion.) Teresa wants a guide who can attend to individual persons in their actual state in a particular moment in time, not one who has a cookie-cutter approach or who jumps to conclusions without the good judgment to recognize where the person actually finds him- or herself. But, at the same time, Teresa also means a spiritual quality that comes from both experience and reflection on it—one's own and that of others. A discerning guide knows the ways of the Spirit and can help a person to discern that movement in his or her own life. Teresa is therefore speaking of a kind of personal, emotional, moral, and spiritual maturity.

Spiritual direction takes place within a relationship, and Teresa's writings reveal that some of her most fruitful direction was the result of longtime and mutually respectful and affectionate relationships.[2] As much as a guide may have a special gift of discernment, it is just such a relationship that

2. Aniano Álvarez-Suárez, "Acompañamiento espiritual," in *Diccionario de Santa Teresa*, ed. Tomás Álvarez, 2nd ed. (Burgos, Spain: Editorial Monte Carmelo, 2006), 17.

fosters both understanding in the guide and trust in the one accompanied. Teresa of Jesus was a profoundly relational person, and good direction served her most fundamental relationship: with God. Her classic definition of prayer reveals both the relational nature of prayer as well as the necessity for a broader growth in conformity to God's will, which, as we have seen, is the Christian life's most fundamental goal:

> For mental prayer in my opinion is nothing else than an intimate sharing between friends; it means taking time frequently to be alone with Him who we know loves us. In order that love be true and the friendship endure, the wills of the friends must be in accord. The will of the Lord, it is already known, cannot be at fault; our will is vicious, sensual, and ungrateful. And if you do not yet love Him as He loves you because you have not reached the degree of conformity with His will, you will endure this pain of spending a long while with one who is so different from you when you see how much it benefits you to possess His friendship and how much He loves you. (L 8.5)

Spiritual direction is a relationship that serves this foundational relationship with God—of which prayer is an essential but not exclusive element. The context of a truly interpersonal and mutual relationship aids the guide in being attentive to a real individual person in actual circumstances.

With counsel that Teresa would undoubtedly have applied to spiritual guides, addressing prioresses in the *Foundations*, she cautions them to exercise discernment in directing the growth of each of the nuns:

The prioress must not then think that she understands a soul at once. Let her leave this to God, for it is He alone who can understand it. Rather, the prioress should strive to guide each nun along the way His Majesty is leading that one, provided that the nun is not failing in obedience or in the more essential matters of the rule and constitutions. (F 18.9)

As with the other two characteristics, we can learn a great deal by remembering Teresa's own experience with spiritual guides who lacked the quality under discussion. We recall here the lack of discerning guidance offered by the otherwise sincere and highly regarded diocesan priest Gaspar Daza in Teresa's early experience of deep prayer:

In this way I arranged that the priest I said was such a servant of God would come to speak to me. This gentleman [Salcedo] was a great friend of that priest whom I thought I could take as my confessor and master. When he brought him to speak to me, I was most embarrassed to find myself in the presence of so holy a man, and I gave him an account of my soul and my prayer; but I didn't want him to hear my confession. I told him I was very busy—and that was true. He began with a holy determination to guide me as though I were a strong person—for by rights I should have been so because of the prayer he observed I was experiencing—in order that I might in no way offend God. When I saw him at once so determined about little things that, as I say, I didn't have the fortitude to give up immediately and so perfectly, I was afflicted. Since I saw he was taking my soul's attachments as something I would have to die to all at once, I realized there was need for much more caution.

In sum, I understood that the means he gave me were not the ones by which I could remedy my situation, because they were suited to a more perfect soul. As for myself, even though I was advanced in receiving favors from God, I was very much at the beginning with regard to virtues and mortification. Certainly, if I were to have had no one else but him to speak to, I believe my soul would never have improved. For the affliction I felt in seeing that I did not do—nor did it seem I could do—that which he told me would have been enough to make me lose hope and give up everything.

I sometimes marvel that God was not pleased that this priest, being a person who has a particular grace for beginning to lead souls to God, understand my soul and take charge of it. I see that what happened was all for my greater good, that I might get to know and deal with people as holy as are those of the Society of Jesus. (L 23.8–9)

Although Gaspar Daza had pushed her without due discretion, she praised another, the Jesuit Baltasar Álvarez who challenged and pushed her in ways that she experienced as difficult at the time—so much so that she was tempted to seek another director. But, in hindsight, she saw that this guide knew how and when to prudently push her according to what she needed and of what she was capable, even though it was not fully apparent to her at the time:

I had a confessor who mortified me very much and was sometimes an affliction and great trial to me because he disturbed me exceedingly, and he was the one who profited me the most as far as I can tell. And although I had a great love for him, I had some temptations to leave him because it seemed to me the affliction he caused me hindered my prayer. Every time that I was determined to change, I then heard that I should not do so and a rebuke that grieved me more than the confessor did. Sometimes I grew weary: on the one hand I was questioning and on the other hand being rebuked—all was necessary because my will did not easily bend. The Lord told me once that it wasn't obedience if I wasn't resolved to suffer, that I should fix my eyes on what He suffered, and that all would be easy. (L 26.3)

The spiritual guide must be able to discern when to push a little and when, on the other hand, to hold back. But the prudent director should not always err on the side of being excessively cautious or timid, because he or she should strive to help the person to advance: "So few and so rare are the spiritual masters who are not excessively discreet in these matters that I believe it is one of the main reasons why beginners do not advance more rapidly to high perfection" (L 13.6).

Discernment or discretion in the spiritual guide respects the freedom of the Holy Spirit and of the person being accompanied. Following the unhelpful experience of direction with Daza, Teresa recounts that the Jesuit rector in Avila instructed Álvarez to guide her with discretion and freedom of spirit, letting "the Spirit of the Lord work":

The new rector didn't restrain my confessor, but rather told him to console me; that there was no reason for fear, and not to lead me by so confining a path; that he should let the spirit of the Lord work, for at times it seemed with these great spiritual impulses that my soul couldn't even breathe. (L 33.8)

In fact, following a conversation with the Jesuit rector himself, Teresa felt immediately comfortable and understood at a profound level because she recognized in him a person of authentic discernment: "I immediately understood his style and saw that his soul was a pure and holy one and that he had a special gift from the Lord for discerning spirits [*don particular del Señor para conocer espíritus*]" (L 33.10).

The movements of God are often quite subtle. As Teresa says: "Like a good shepherd, with a whistle so gentle that even they themselves almost fail to hear it, He makes them recognize His voice" (IC 4.3.2). A good director, then, must be able to attend to the subtle movements of the Spirit and especially to help the other person to do so. In this sense, respecting the actual situation of this particular individual, a good director must leave the person free to attend and respond to God as they are able and ready. This was the case in another of Teresa's early Jesuit directors, Diego de Cetina:

> As a consequence I began to make many changes, although the confessor didn't press me; rather it seemed that he thought all the changes of little importance. And this urged me more because he guided my soul by stressing the love of God and allowed freedom and used no pressure if I didn't set about doing things out of love. (L 24.1)

A particular problem mentioned often by Teresa is what she called melancholy (what we today would probably call depression)—both in her books (e.g., IC 3.1.6; 6.2.1–2, 5; 6.8.3) and frequently in her letters (e.g., LE 69.4; 98.8; 149.2; 231.7). She devotes significant attention to the problem in the *Foundations* (4–8). In small, enclosed communities, in a time before counseling and psychological screening, this must have been a frequent and significant problem. But of particular importance to the spiritual life is the ability to prudently distinguish melancholy from aridity or dryness in prayer and other spiritual states (IC 6.2.5). Such prudence, Teresa warns, is not the same as an excess of caution, grounded in a guide's lack of personal experience of both the more typical trials and ways of God in advancing persons in prayer. In her own experience, excessive caution can lead to a too facile "diagnosis" of either melancholy or the work of the devil (IC 6.1.8).

In the end, a good spiritual guide must be prudent enough to be able to recognize his or her own limits and so guide the other with a discreet humility:

> With his humility he will do more good for souls and for himself than by becoming a contemplative without it. For I repeat that if he doesn't have experience and a very great deal of humility in knowing that he doesn't understand the experience, but that it's not impossible on that account, he will be of little profit to himself and of still less profit to those with whom he deals. If he's humble, he shouldn't fear that the Lord will allow either of them to be deceived. (L 34.12)

All Three Qualities

The ideal, of course, is to find a spiritual guide who possesses all three of the characteristics highlighted by Teresa. In fact, they are interrelated. While prudence or discretion is a natural quality and an acquired virtue, in spiritual matters, it is enhanced by knowledge of theology and the wisdom of spiritual masters and by experience. In fact, more broadly, the virtue of prudence itself grows by practice and experience. A sustained personal relationship with God and deep prayer yields its own spiritual wisdom, which gives a sometimes more authentic insight into whatever has been learned academically about theology or spirituality. And, without some formal study of theology and classic spirituality, a spiritual guide can fail to help a person to interpret their experience and so, to some degree, to form it in keeping with an authentic Christian tradition. Teresa invites us to look for a spiritual guide with all three qualities.

Chapter Five

Teresa of Avila, Director of Others

Teresa, herself directed by many, became a learned, experienced, and prudent director of others. A profoundly relational person, she was inherently a woman of great insight and intelligence. In her own long spiritual journey, she had personal experience of the ups and downs of prayer, the determination and discipline required to grow in a true relationship with God, and knowledge of the difficulty of discerning the movement of the Spirit and God's will. She was, of course, a woman of deep prayer and profound spiritual experience. But, more, she came to understand her experience and how to describe it to others, which she herself notes is not usually present in one person: "For it is one grace to receive the Lord's favor; another, to understand which favor and grace it is; and a third, to know how to describe and explain it" (L 17.5). And, as we have seen, Teresa came to experience many different spiritual guides, both good and bad. All of this—her personal gifts, her own prayer, and her experience of direction, together surely with her own openness to the working of the Holy Spirit—made her a learned, experienced, and prudent director for others. Perhaps we hear a hint of her own experience when she writes: "It seems to me that one of the greatest consolations a person can have on earth must be to see other souls helped through his own efforts" (M 7.6).

Spiritual Direction in Writing

Like John of the Cross, Teresa's writings are a form of direction. This is, in fact, even more evident in her case since her style is so often colloquial, so full of images, direct, and practical. She offers counsel about things that she herself experienced, about what others have asked her, what she had observed, and what she had read or learned from others. By the time she began to write her major works, she was already well advanced in the spiritual life. Teresa was therefore able not only to describe but also to offer counsel about pitfalls and helps on the entire length of the spiritual journey. Her writings often read like an experienced guide along a well-travelled but long road who offers maps, directions, descriptions, cautions, and practical tips for the journey, both to the novice traveler and to the seasoned pilgrim.

Even a book like her *Foundations* is filled with counsel on prayer—but not without recognition of the practical complexities of finding an appropriate balance between prayer and necessary work:

> And I thus was sorry for them to see they were so occupied
> with so many business matters and things that obedience com-

manded them. I was thinking to myself, and even said so, that it wasn't possible in the midst of such commotion for the spirit to grow, for at that time they didn't have much spirit. O Lord, how different are Your paths from our clumsy imaginings! And how from a soul that is already determined to love You and is abandoned into Your hands, You do not want anything but that it obey, that it inquire well into what is for Your greater service, and that it desire this! There's no need for it to be seeking out paths or choosing them, for its will is Yours. You, my Lord, take up this care of guiding it to where it receives the most benefit. The prelate who is the superior may not be concerned for what benefits the soul but concerned only that the business he thinks is fitting for the community be attended to. Yet, You, my God, do have concern and go about disposing the soul and the things with which it is dealing in such a way that, without understanding how, we find in ourselves spiritual improvement, so great that we are afterward left amazed.

There was a person to whom I spoke a few days ago who for about fifteen years was kept so busy through obedience with work in occupations and government that in all those years he didn't remember having had one day for himself, although he tried the best he could to keep a pure conscience and have some periods each day for prayer. His soul in its inclination is one of the most obedient I have seen, and so he communicates this spirit of obedience to all those with whom he deals. The Lord has repaid him well; for he has found that he has, without knowing how, that same precious and desirable liberty of spirit that the perfect have. (F 5.6–7)

Clearly, whatever help a spiritual companion might offer must attend to the particular vocation and actual life situation of the individual person.

Teresa's many extant letters, as we will see below, show her giving spiritual advice to her nuns, to friars and to bishops, and to laymen and laywomen. Among her published books, it is the *Way of Perfection* that shows her most especially engaged in a type of spiritual direction. The book is intended as a sort of primer in prayer, addressed to her nuns who had asked for her instruction. And she is certainly teaching, but, no less, she is offering practical counsel on the ordinary events and relationships within her monasteries—really, ordinary human realities such as taking needless offense from the words or actions of others, praying in time of illness, and mutual service in community. Although she would come to address topics of deep prayer, the *Way* shows that her counsel is directed far more broadly at life in general. The Christian journey that she is laying out for her readers is not simply about prayer but about living, relating to others, and being transformed through prayer, which she defines foundationally as a relationship of friendship with God (L 8.5).

Though Teresa is usually describing her own experience and wisdom, she is quite aware as she writes that not everyone is led by the Spirit in exactly the same way. And, as a wise director herself, she freely acknowledges it:

> It is not my intention or thought that what I say here be taken for certain and as an infallible rule, for that would be foolish in things so difficult. Since there are many paths along this way of the spirit, it could be that I will manage to say certain useful things about some of them. If those who do not walk along the path of which I'm speaking do not understand what I'm saying, it will be because they are walking by another. (F 5.1)

"God," she says elsewhere, "doesn't lead all by one path" (W 17.2). And as she leads her reader through the seven dwelling places of the *Interior Castle*, she regularly notes that there are many rooms in each of these dwellings—signaling that not everyone's experience will be the same (IC 1.1.3; 5.3.4; 5.5.2; 7.2.1; Epil.3).

Some of Teresa's "Directees"

One of the people that Teresa first accompanied in the ways of prayer was her own father. This began during the time before her own mature "conversion" and while she was herself going through a period of infidelity to the deeper prayer that she had already begun to practice earlier. She describes the help she offered her father, which clearly included elements of teaching, counsel, and encouragement. But she also served as a spiritual companion during times of trial in his life:

> Since I loved my father so much, I desired for him the good I felt I got out of the practice of prayer. It seemed to me that in this life there could be no greater good than the practice of prayer. So in roundabout ways, as much as I could, I began to strive to get him to pray. I gave him books for this purpose. Since he had such virtue, as I mentioned, he settled into this practice so well that within five or six years—it seems it was— he was so advanced that I praised the Lord very much, and this gave me the greatest consolation. Very severe were the many kinds of trials he had; all of them he suffered with the deepest conformity to God's will. He came often to see me, for it consoled him to speak of the things of God. (L 7.10)

In his final illness, she offered counsel that seemed to give him peace in enduring his final sufferings and enabled him to die in peace:

> I told him that since he was so devoted to the memory of when the Lord carried the burden of the cross that His Majesty thought He would like to make him experience something of what He suffered with that pain. This comforted my father so much that it seems to me I never heard him complain again. (L 7.16)

And it was at this time that the Dominican Vicente Barrón, who had been confessor to her father, became perhaps her first true director (L 7.16–17).

But this early ministry of spiritual accompaniment Teresa offered to her father—apparently with some success—also extended to others as well:

> He wasn't the only one; I also tried to get some other persons to practice prayer. Even though I was taking part in these vanities, when I saw others who were fond of praying, I told them how to practice meditation and assisted them and gave them books. For, from the time I began prayer, as I said, I had this desire that others serve God. (L 7.13)

Also in the *Life*, we see Teresa offering spiritual guidance to two noblewomen who became both benefactors and friends, often in the context of sharing her own experiences. With Luisa de la Cerda, we get a sense of this relationship from their first meeting when Teresa was sent to comfort the widow but became a true spiritual friend and companion (L 34.1–5;

see also L 24.6; 30.3). In the same way, we see in Teresa's friendship with Guiomar de Ulloa a relationship of true spiritual companionship (L.24.4; 30.3; 34.18).

It is in her letters, however, that we especially see Teresa, the spiritual guide, at work—teaching, offering counsel, and sometimes chastising.[1] Below we will quote from a number of these letters in order to show especially the mature experience but also the discerning spirit with which she writes to nuns, priests, laity, and family. She counsels one of her prioresses:

> Your manner of prayer makes me happy. Recognizing that you have it and that God is doing you a favor is not a lack of humility since you understand that it is not your doing but his. That is how we know that the prayer is from God. I greatly praise him that you are faring so well, and I will try to give him joyful thanks as you ask me. Ask God that I might be the kind of person whose prayers he will answer. (LE 188.4 of November 11, 1576, to María de San José)

She encourages a nun who was physically and inwardly distressed:

> Concerning what you say about your interior life, the greater the disturbance the less attention you should pay to it, for it clearly proceeds from a weak imagination and bad humor; and since the devil sees this, he adds his bit. But have no fear,

1. Marcel Lépée, "Spiritual Direction in the Letters of St. Teresa," in *Carmelite Studies I: Spiritual Direction*, ed. John Sullivan (Washington, DC: ICS Publications, 1980), 61–80.

for St. Paul says that God will not permit us to be tempted beyond what we can bear. And even though it may seem that you give consent, it's not so; rather, you will benefit from all of this. Continue with your cure, for love of God, and try to eat well, and don't remain alone thinking about nothing. Seek some diversion inasmuch as you can and however possible. I would like to be there, for there's much I would talk about for your entertainment. (LE 143.8 of November 2, 1576, to María Bautista)

But her letters show that Teresa's spiritual guidance extended beyond her father and her nuns. To a priest who would later become an archbishop, Teresa wrote:

With regard to the desire you experience to cut short your prayer, pay no attention to it. Instead praise the Lord for the desire you have for prayer and believe that this is what your will wants—and love to be with God. Melancholy dislikes being treated with severity. It is best to use less severe means and at times relax outdoors where you can walk and see the sky; your prayer will suffer no loss because of this; it's necessary that we bear our weakness and not try to constrain our nature. Everything amounts to seeking God, since it is for him that we search out every kind of means, and the soul must be led gently. (LE 69.4 of July 3, 1574, to Teutonio de Braganza)

She advises a widower, in a letter written sometime in 1574:

I would need more time to answer your question—I mean about what touches on prayer—although the substance of the answer is that this is a very common way of proceeding by those who have reached contemplation. I have often told you this, but you forget it. You have to realize that just as there are different seasons on this earth, so there are in the interior life, and it cannot be otherwise. So don't be troubled—you are not at fault. As for the rest, I cannot be a judge, since I am an interested party; and also my natural inclination has always been toward the state of solitude, although I have not merited to have it, and since this is the state proper to our order, I could be giving counsel appropriate for myself but not for what is fitting for you. Speak about this clearly with Father Rector [the Jesuit Baltazar Álvarez] and he will see what is best; and try observing to which one your spirit has the greater leaning. May God keep you, for I am writing so many letters that I don't know how I have been able to say this much, and the messenger is waiting. (LE 75.1–2 to Antonio Gaytán)

Teresa had a multilayered relationship with the Carmelite friar Jeronimo Gracián. Thirty years her junior, he was the first provincial of the Discalced Carmelites and thus, for a time, her superior. She had promised to obey him in everything. He, at the same time, was a friend and a counselor. Sometimes she took a maternal tone toward him. And at other times, she functioned as a spiritual guide for him, though she recognized that some might wonder about the appropriateness of his self-revelation to her:

It will seem inappropriate that he should have informed me of so many personal matters about his soul. Perhaps the Lord wanted this that I might record it here, and He might be praised in His creatures. For I know that neither to any confessor nor to any other person has this Father manifested so much about himself. At times he had reason for so doing because he thought that on account of my age and from what he had heard about me I had some experience. It was while we were speaking about other matters that he told me about these things and additional ones that cannot be suitably put in writing, for I would be going on at much greater length. (F 23.11)

In an early letter to him—before the separation of the Calced and Discalced, using code names for fear of the letters being intercepted—she advises him about his experience of prayer (LE 136.4–5 of October 23, 1576). In other letters, she cautions him about moderation and the need for adequate rest (LE 174.2–3 of January 9, 1577, and LE 311.2 of October 4, 1579).

Teresa's spiritual counsel included not only her father but also other members of her extended family. To a second cousin, she wrote:

You shouldn't be surprised that you are not able to be very recollected in the midst of so many difficulties. That would be impossible. If you return to your good rule of life when they pass, I will be content. Please God that all goes very well with you, but do not be concerned about having more or having less, for even if a great deal is left for you, everything will soon come to an end. (LE 153.2 of November 26, 1576, to Luis de Cepeda)

She counseled a niece ("Teresita") who had entered Carmel and who shared her name:

As for the dryness, it seems to me that the Lord is now treating you as one who is strong. He wants to try you in order to know the love you have for him, whether it is present in dryness as well as in spiritual delights. Take it as a very great favor from God. Don't let it cause you any grief, for perfection does not consist in delight but in the virtues. When you least expect, devotion will return.

As for what you say about that sister, try not to think of it, but turn away from the thought. And don't think that when a thought comes into your mind, even if it concerns something very bad, you are immediately at fault, for the thought is nothing. I too would like to see that sister experience the same dryness, for I don't know if she understands herself, and for her own good we could desire this. When some bad thought comes to you, bless yourself, or recite an Our Father, or strike your breast and try to think of something else, and you will instead be meriting because you will be resisting. (LE 351.2–3 of August 7, 1580, to Teresa de Jesús)

But perhaps the clearest example of the spiritual guidance that Teresa offered in her letters is her correspondence with her own brother Lorenzo, who was a regular benefactor of her foundations. In one letter (LE 177 of January 17, 1577), for example, she reluctantly accepts the role as his spiritual guide while refusing to accept a promise of obedience from him. She comments on his reported experience and practice of prayer, offering clarifications, teaching, and counsel. She offers prudent advice about ascetical practice and addressing his experience of more carnal desire. But, at the same time, the letter concerns such mundane topics as his gift of sardines, advice about his physical health, and financial matters. In another letter (LE 182 of February 10, 1577), she again comments on his experience of prayer and gives him prudent advice about the value but also of the need for real moderation in ascetical practices so as not to harm his health. In fact, this letter is a particular illustration of Teresa's own prudent and discerning spirit as a guide. And, as a final example, we see that in a third letter (LE 185 of February 27–28, 1577), she again offers discerning counsel about the ascetical practices that would be appropriate to his particular health and encourages him in some experience of dryness in his prayer. She encourages him to understanding for their brother Pedro.

The varied writings of Teresa of Jesus show that she herself came to be what she desired in those who offered guidance to her—learned, experienced, and discerning. In addition to her own considerable natural gifts, she had learned from directors, both good and bad. She had grown accustomed to attending to the movements of the Spirit. She herself had long walked the ways of prayer. As friend, companion, superior, and leader, she had learned to read and to accept—to embrace and to challenge—human nature as it is. The testimonies given for her beatification and canonization reveal that her contemporaries were profoundly aware and deeply blessed by her guidance—an awareness that continues to our own day.

Chapter Six

Direction for
a Holistic Spirituality

Teresa of Jesus is rightly renowned as a teacher of prayer, and her major works provide classic descriptions and explanations of the deepest prayer experiences. Perhaps it would be easy to assume that her understanding of spiritual direction would therefore be focused exclusively on the topic of prayer. But Teresa's spirituality was not disembodied, cut off from the ordinary events and interactions of daily life. She wrote about the path of contemplative and mystical prayer, because there were so few resources available to her nuns and to their close lay associates. But her books and letters reveal a woman with her feet firmly planted on the ground and a spirituality very much rooted in the ordinary. This is not the place to attempt a full examination of her embodied, holistic spirituality, but we must understand that, for Teresa, the Christian life is more than prayer—as must be the spiritual guidance that supports it.

In an earlier chapter, we noted the contemporary dissatisfaction with the term "spiritual direction." "Direction" can seem to suggest that those seeking guidance or accompaniment surrender their own freedom to the authority or the presumed wisdom of the guide. The word "spiritual," for its part, can seem to suggest that the subject matter of the relationship and conversation is narrowly or exclusively about prayer and transcendent relationship with God, cut off from ordinary life and relationships. But the guidance offered by Teresa, the great mystic and teacher of prayer, is by no means "spiritual," in this narrow sense. All of her works reveal her active involvement in and concern for relationships, ordinary daily activities, and the broader common life of her nuns. In fact, she famously advised her nuns that "the Lord walks among the pots and pans" (F 5.8). God, then, could be found, not only in periods of quiet prayer, but also there in the kitchen where the nuns served each other in ordinary ways.

When she wrote the *Way of Perfection*—intended as a kind of primer on prayer—Teresa intentionally devoted the first half of the work to speaking of essential virtues that must ground a life of prayer. These virtues, as she describes them—humility, detachment, and love of others—are practical and remain essential at every stage of the Christian journey. They are different aspects of the holistic transformation that feeds and is fed by deepening prayer. In a similar way, in the *Interior Castle*, Teresa describes an inner journey of prayer, self-awareness, and deep relationship with God. But although her focus there is the experience and description of prayer, she presupposes the broader transformation of life that must occur at every stage along the way. This perspective becomes clear in the critical image of the silkworm, which begins as an ugly worm but is transformed into a beautiful butterfly (IC 5.2–3). This is a metaphor for a life transformation that is far broader than growth in prayer, no matter how profound.[1]

Teresa speaks frequently of the gospel sisters, Martha and Mary—Martha traditionally understood to represent the active life and Mary, the contemplative. Jesus, we recall, said that Mary had chosen the better part, resulting in the popular conclusion that the contemplative life is the higher. Again, it might be assumed that Teresa of Jesus, teacher of mystical prayer, would continue this traditional viewpoint. But she reminds us instead that Martha and Mary were, in fact, sisters who lived and worked together. In our lives too, these two sisters—that is, the active and the contemplative dimensions of our Christian journey—must walk hand-in-hand (IC 7.4; W 31.5; M 7.3; ST 59.5), each of us according to our distinctive calling. Further, she says, even if Martha never attained true contemplative prayer, we must recall that she is nonetheless *Saint* Martha and is now in heaven (W 17.5–6). When the person finally arrives at the innermost dwellings of the interior castle and attains the transforming union with God, the person discovers that the fundamental challenge is not solitary retreat but rather practical works of love for others (IC 7.4.6)— Martha and Mary now working in complete harmony.

1. See Mark O'Keefe, *The Way of Transformation: Saint Teresa of Avila on the Foundation and Fruit of Prayer* (Washington, DC: ICS Publications, 2016), 167–72. As commentators have noted, the image should actually be a caterpillar rather than a silkworm.

As much as Teresa wrote about mystical prayer, she is emphatic that extraordinary experiences are not the ultimate goal of either Christian prayer or the Christian life. The fundamental goal, for her, is conformity to the will of God. Mystical experiences can be helpful in promoting this congruence between our wills and that of God—with every mystical grace, Teresa herself reported growth in virtue—but such experiences are neither necessary nor the height of the Christian life. As she says:

> The whole aim of any person who is beginning prayer—and don't forget this, because it's very very important—should be that he work and prepare himself with determination and every possible effort to bring his will into conformity with God's will. Be certain that, as I shall say later, the greatest perfection attainable along the spiritual path lies in this conformity. It is the person who lives in more perfect conformity who will receive more from the Lord and be more advanced on this road. Don't think that in what concerns perfection there is some mystery or things unknown or still to be understood, for in perfect conformity to God's will lies all our good. (IC 2.1.8)

This is a fundamental belief that she repeats elsewhere:

> The highest perfection obviously does not consist in interior delights or in great raptures or in visions or in the spirit of prophecy but in having our will so much in conformity with God's will that there is nothing we know He wills that we do not want with all our desire, and in accepting the bitter as happily as we do the delightful when we know that His Majesty desires it. (F 5.10)

We recall the great emphasis that Teresa of Avila places on self-knowledge. She tells us at the beginning of the *Interior Castle* that the entrance to this great edifice (which is our soul) requires prayer and self-knowledge. And this knowledge of self involves knowing our sin and our need but also—and more fundamentally—that, created in the image of God, every human person is more precious and wondrous than can be imagined:

> It is that we consider our soul to be like a castle made entirely out of a diamond or of very clear crystal, in which there are many rooms, just as in heaven there are many dwelling places. For in reflecting upon it carefully, Sisters, we realize that the soul of the just person is nothing else but a paradise where the Lord says He finds His delight. So then, what do you think that abode will be like where a King so powerful, so wise, so pure, so full of all good things takes His delight? I don't find anything comparable to the magnificent beauty of a soul and its marvelous capacity. Indeed, our intellects, however keen, can hardly comprehend it, just as they cannot comprehend God; but He Himself says that He created us in His own image and likeness. (IC 1.1.1)

A spiritual guide assists us in the entire journey—in growing in prayer and in self-knowledge, in coming to know God and to know ourselves as we are: profoundly beautiful and precious as well as sinful and in need of divine mercy. This is a challenging and multidimensional journey in which it is all too easy to be self-deceived.

It is true that Teresa's reflection on spiritual guidance often focuses on the distinctive guidance of contemplatives. This only makes sense in light of her immediate intended audience of first-generation, fervent nuns of the Discalced reform and their supporters. She is, as we have said, writing on contemplative and mystical prayer because she sees the need to fill a gap, and her teaching is based on her own profound experiences of prayer. But none of this should lead us to believe that spiritual guidance—and the necessary qualities of directors—is restricted to prayer. Her spiritual vision is too broad and incarnational to restrict the important assistance offered by a good spiritual guide in that way.

Part Three

John of the Cross

John of the Cross was twenty-seven years younger than Teresa of Jesus. In terms of such things as formal academic education, personality, social background, and manner of written expression, they were very different. John was male, a priest, and university trained. Teresa was female in an age and culture that looked down on women. She was bright, literate, and ultimately well-read but lacking a formal education. Their personal experience of society and church was quite different because of their different horizons. And yet, they were like-minded partners in the Discalced Carmelite reform that Teresa had initiated. For a time, John was Teresa's confessor and spiritual director, but their mutual influence on each other seems abundantly clear in their writings. Their vision of the spiritual life and the Christian journey is largely the same (even if their expressions of it often seem quite different). And so is their understanding of the essential qualities that a good spiritual director should possess. Both of them—in their distinctive ways—manifested those characteristics in their own direction of others. We will see in the chapters in this third part that John embraces the same three essential characteristics of a good spiritual director—learned, experienced, and discerning—though perhaps with different emphases.

The reader will note in the longer citations from the works of John of the Cross that his written style is quite different from that of Teresa. Teresa's writing is more descriptive, more conversational, and more personal. John's is often more formal and analytical—and this is particularly the case in the prose commentaries on his poetry, from which the longer quotes here are drawn. Yet, it is clear that John is speaking from experience, and his purpose is to serve as a practical aid to directors and directed alike. While many readers have found John's style to be initially off-putting or intimidating, no one can doubt the depths of his insights, whether about spiritual direction or about the spiritual journey more broadly.

Chapter Seven

John of the Cross, Spiritual Director in Person and in Writing

John of the Cross, mystic and mystical writer, also had an active life of ministry. He was one of the first male collaborators with Teresa of Jesus in the Discalced Carmelite reform. He traveled across Spain, making foundations of men and assisting in the establishment of communities of Discalced nuns. He held important offices among the Discalced friars—busy as a superior, visitator, and formator. Beyond the particular work of the Order, he was a dedicated and frequent preacher. But his main ministry was as a spiritual director—to nuns and friars, *beatas* (laywomen living a life of prayer and service without formal religious profession), laywomen and laymen, professors and students at the universities of Alcalá and Baeza, young and old, at different points on the spiritual journey and along the path of prayer, from different social classes in a highly stratified society.[1] One Carmelite author says of John: "The whole apostolic life of St. John of the Cross was concentrated upon the exercise of spiritual direction."[2] Another summarizes: "His principal ministry was spiritual direction."[3] A well-known contemporary Jesuit spiritual writer, Thomas Green, says of John that he was "perhaps the greatest spiritual director the church has known"![4] He goes on to say that he himself annually rereads the teaching on direction that John offers in the *Living Flame* (F 3.27–67) in order to keep himself honest as a spiritual director.

But undoubtedly John's principal spiritual guidance was offered to nuns—a ministry that began in earnest during the five years in which he served as confessor-director at the Monastery of the Incarnation in Avila. The monastery, in which Teresa had professed before her foundation of St. Joseph, had not joined her Discalced reform. But Teresa had been ordered there by the Carmelite provincial as prioress—against her own

1. See especially Dennis Graviss, *Portrait of the Spiritual Director in the Writings of Saint John of the Cross*, 2nd ed. (Rome, Italy: Edizioni Carmelitane, 2014), and Kevin Culligan, "Toward a Model of Spiritual Direction Based on the Writings of Saint John of the Cross and Carl Rogers: An Exploratory Study" (PhD diss., Boston University Graduate School, 1979).

2. Gabriel of St. Mary Magdalen, *The Spiritual Director According to the Principles of St. John of the Cross* (Westminster, MD: Newman Press, 1952), 13.

3. Graviss, *Portrait of the Spiritual Director*, 9.

4. Thomas H. Green, *The Friend of the Bridegroom: Spiritual Direction and the Encounter with Christ* (Notre Dame, IN: Ave Maria Press, 2000), 72.

wishes and those of the nuns—in order to address a number of internal problems. Beyond their resentment at the loss of their right to elect their own superior, the nuns feared that the imposition of Teresa as their prioress would force them into the reform. Teresa, however, proved to be balanced and prudent. In the same way, when Teresa arranged to have John brought there as confessor, the nuns feared his reputation for austerity and rigor. But they found him gentle and discerning. It was this experience—in which he also directed Teresa herself—that must have served as a kind of apprenticeship for the years of spiritual guidance of nuns that lay ahead.

When John was later sent to found and lead communities of friars in Andalusia in southern Spain, one of his principal priorities was to serve as confessor and guide to Discalced nuns at Beas, Caravaca, and Granada. For those ten years, he demonstrated his commitment to this ministry by traveling great distances on foot along bad roads, back and forth, even in the midst of his many responsibilities among the friars as founder and superior. Returning eventually to his native Castille in northern Spain, he continued this spiritual direction ministry to the nuns in Segovia. A number of his few extant letters, as we will see below, were letters of spiritual guidance for nuns. Many of the brief *Sayings of Light and Love* too were brief lessons intended for the nuns under his guidance.

We know that John's ministry as a spiritual guide was deeply appreciated and highly regarded, as the testimonies given during the process of his beatification demonstrate.[5]

---

5. Graviss, *Portrait of the Spiritual Director*, 154–55; Culligan, "Toward a Model," 80–82.

But surely his most prominent praise is offered by none other than Teresa of Jesus herself who admired his skills as a director and his personal witness to the life of the spirit and prayer. In a letter to her close associate Mother Anne of Jesus who had not been impressed at her first meeting with John and took offense that he had dared to refer to Teresa of Jesus as his spiritual daughter, Teresa wrote:

> I was amused, daughter, at how groundless is your complaining, for you have in your very midst *mi padre* [emphasis in original] Fray John of the Cross, a heavenly and divine man. I tell you, daughter, from the time he left and went down there I have not found anyone in all Castile like him, or anyone who communicates so much fervor for walking along the way to heaven. You will not believe the feeling of loneliness that his absence causes me. Realize what a great treasure you have there in that saint. All the nuns in your house should speak and communicate with him on matters concerning their souls, and they will see how beneficial it is. They will find themselves making much progress in all that pertains to spirituality and perfection, for our Lord has given him a special grace in this regard.
>
> I declare to you that I would be most happy to have my father Fray John of the Cross here, *who truly is the father of my soul* [emphasis added] and one from whom it benefited most in its conversations with him. Speak with him, my daughters, in total simplicity, for I assure you that you can do so as though you were speaking with me. This will bring you great satisfaction, for he is a very spiritual man with much experience and learning. Those here who were formed by his teaching miss him greatly. Give thanks to God who has ordained that you have him there so close. I am writing to tell him to look after

you, and I know from his great charity that he will do so, whatever be your need. (LE 277, November–December 1578)[6]

Similarly, in a letter to Mother Ana de San Alberto, Teresa wrote: "Daughter, Father John of the Cross is going there. Let the nuns in that monastery speak to him of matters concerning their souls with simplicity as though they were speaking with me, for he has the spirit of our Lord" (LE 323, January 1580). Likewise, in a letter to her brother Lorenzo (one example of her letters of spiritual direction to him), she commented: "I rejoiced that you feel that Fray John understands you, for he has experience" (LE 177, January 17, 1577).

In a number of other letters, Teresa attests as well more generally to John's sanctity. Writing to King Philip II of Spain, trying to gain John's release from his imprisonment by the Calced friars, she says: "He is so great a servant of our Lord that the nuns are truly edified, and this city is amazed by the remarkable amount of good he has done there, and so they consider him a saint; and in my opinion he is one and has been one all his life" (LE 218, December 4, 1577). To an important friend and supporter, Teresa wrote: "One of them,

6. In the ICS edition of Teresa's *Letters*, Kavanaugh comments on this letter: "It is not certain whether these two fragments (nos. 1 and 2) belong to the same letter. The text comes from the process for the beatification of St. John of the Cross. At the end of October, the saint began his ministry in Andalusia as prior of the monastery of El Calvario, not far from Beas." Kieran Kavanaugh, trans., *The Collected Letters of St. Teresa of Avila*, vol. 2 (Washington, DC: ICS Publications, 2007), 145.

at least, whose name is Fray John of the Cross, is considered a saint by everyone, men and women alike, and I don't think they exaggerate. In my opinion, he is a gem" (LE 266 to Don Teutonio de Braganza on January 16, 1578). And to yet another prioress, Teresa comments: "My daughter: I am very sorry about Sister Isabel's sickness. I am sending you the saintly Fray John of the Cross, for God has given him the grace to cast out devils from persons having them. Just recently here in Avila he has driven out three legions of devils from a person, demanding that they identify themselves, and they obeyed at once. What they fear in him is so much grace accompanied by so much humility" (LE 51 to Mother Inés de Jesús in May 1573).

Writing as Direction

Beyond the spiritual guidance offered in person, John's writings were intended as a form of spiritual direction. This is true even of his major prose works—the *Ascent*, *Dark Night*, *Spiritual Canticle*, and *Living Flame*—although they may appear at times to be intended as academic treatises on ascetical and mystical theology. They were written, rather, as a form of spiritual teaching and practical guidance for the nuns and laywomen that he directed but could not see for long periods of time. The major works are commentaries on his mystical poetry, written at the persistent request of his directees. Especially in the *Ascent* and *Dark Night*, we see John actually offering explicit spiritual counsel, with occasional comments on how a good director ought to guide a person (both, we assume, to form the spiritual guides themselves and to give would-be directees a good sense of how a sound guide should accompany them). While John wrote no work directed solely and principally to spiritual direction, it is in the *Living Flame* (3.27–67) that he offers his most focused and lengthiest teaching.

In the prologue of the *Ascent*, John makes clear his intention of providing sound spiritual guidance to those who want to advance quickly in the spiritual life but who otherwise might lack such assistance:

> With God's help, then, we will propose doctrine and counsel for beginners and proficients that they may understand or at least know how to practice abandonment to God's guidance when He wants them to advance. Some spiritual fathers are likely to be a hindrance and harm rather than a help to these souls that journey on this road. Such directors have neither understanding nor experience of these ways. . . . With divine help we will discuss all this: how individuals should behave; what method the confessor should use in dealing with them; signs to recognize this purification of the soul that we call the dark night; whether it is the purification of the senses or of the spirit; and how we can discern whether this affliction is caused by melancholia or some other deficiency of sense or spirit. (A Prol.4, 6)

But it is in the shorter works that we see more clearly and immediately that John's writing is intended as a type of spiritual guidance. And we see, as well, the gentleness and balance that marked his ministry of direction—a spirit that, again, may not seem quite so apparent in his major prose works, notably the *Ascent* and *Dark Night*. The *Precautions* and the *Counsels to a Young Religious* are both clearly works of spiritual guidance for eager nuns and friars in the first fervor of the Discalced reform. The *Sayings of Light and Love* are a collection of little maxims that John wrote out and gave to his directees in order to reinforce and remind them of a particular counsel to be taken to heart. Witnesses attest that this was a frequent practice of John's, and there were undoubtedly far more such maxims than have come down to us in contemporary collections. He opens the collection of these *Sayings* with a prayer that manifests both their purpose of guidance and the gentleness and prudence of his style:

> Lord, you love discretion, you love light, you love love; these three you love above the other operations of the soul. Hence these will be sayings of discretion for the wayfarer, of light for the way, and of love in the wayfaring. May there be nothing of worldly rhetoric in them or the long-winded and dry eloquence of weak and artificial human wisdom, which never pleases you. Let us speak to the heart words bathed in sweetness and love that do indeed please you, removing obstacles and stumbling blocks from the paths of many souls who unknowingly trip and unconsciously walk in the path of error—poor souls who think they are right in what concerns the following of your beloved Son, our Lord Jesus Christ, in becoming like him, imitating his life, actions, and virtues, and the form of his nakedness and purity of spirit. Father of mercies, come to our aid, for without you, Lord, we can do nothing. (SLL Prol.)

John's poetry speaks with sublime passion and longing, revealing him as the inheritor of a long history in the Christian spiritual tradition of a so-called love (bridal or spousal) mysticism. His commentaries make evident his grasp of the Scholastic theology and spirit of his period, his keen mind for analysis and definition, and the unapologetic spiritual fervor that characterized not only himself but also his first readers in the earliest years of the Discalced reform. But it is his letters—the handful of only thirty-three that have come down to us—that reveal his affection, his moderation, his warmth, and his care. Kevin Culligan identifies three particular characteristics manifested by John in the letters (drawn from the qualities that psychologist Carl Rogers said should mark a good therapist): genuineness, caring, and understanding.[7] A Spanish author describes John's style as demanding but, at the same time, clear, simple, profound, and affectionate.[8] These qualities are consistent with the testimonies of the witnesses during the long and much delayed process for his beatification (not finally proclaimed until 1675).

Just a few examples from the *Letters* will give us a flavor of his spiritual direction-in-writing. In a letter to a laywoman, he writes:

> A few days ago I wrote to you . . . in answer to your last letter, which, as was your hope, I prized. I have answered you in that

7. Kevin Culligan, "Qualities of a Good Guide: Spiritual Direction in John of the Cross' Letters," in *Carmelite Studies VI: John of the Cross*, ed. Steven Payne (Washington, DC: ICS Publications, 1992), 65–68.

8. Aniano Álvarez-Suárez, "Dirección espiritual," in *Diccionario de San Juan de la Cruz*, ed. Eulogio Pacho (Burgos, Spain: Editorial Monte Carmelo, 2009), 334.

letter, since I believe I have received all your letters. And I have felt your grief, afflictions, and loneliness. These, in silence, ever tell me so much that the pen cannot declare it. They are all comparable to knocks and rappings at the door of your soul so it might love more, for they cause more prayer and spiritual sighs to God that he might fulfill the soul's petition. I have already told you there is no reason to become disturbed over those little things, but do what they have ordered you to do; and when they impede it, be obedient and let me know of it, for God will provide what is best. God watches over the affairs of those who truly love him without their worrying about them. (L 11 to Juana de Pedraza on January 28, 1589)

John opens a letter to a Discalced friar who has written to him for spiritual counsel:

May the peace of Jesus Christ, my son, be always in your soul. I received Your Reverence's letter in which you told me of the great desires our Lord gives you to occupy your will in him alone by loving him above all things, and in which you asked for some counsels to help you do this. I am happy God has given you such holy desires, and I shall be much happier if you carry them out. In order to do so, you should . . . (L 13 to a Discalced Carmelite friar on April 14, 1589[?])

John's letter to a Discalced nun suffering from scruples (written apparently shortly before Pentecost) shows his gentle but firm, directive but affirming, counsel to a troubled soul:

In these days try to keep interiorly occupied with a desire for the coming of the Holy Spirit and on the feast and afterward with his continual presence. Let your care and esteem for this be so great that nothing else will matter to you or receive your attention, whether it may concern some affliction or some other disturbing memories. And if there be faults in the house during these days, pass over them for love of the Holy Spirit and of what you owe to the peace and quietude of the soul in which he is pleased to dwell.

If you could put an end to your scruples, I think it would be better for your quietude of soul not to confess during these days. But when you do confess, you should do so in this manner:

In regard to thoughts and imaginings (whether they concern judgments, or other inordinate objects or representations, or any other motions) that occur without being desired or accepted or deliberately adverted to: Do not confess them or pay attention to them or worry about them. It is better to forget them no matter how much they afflict the soul. At most you can mention in general any omission or remissness as regards the purity and perfection you ought to have in the interior faculties: memory, intellect, and will.

In regard to words: Confess any want of caution in speaking with truthfulness and rectitude, out of necessity, and with purity of intention.

In regard to deeds: Confess any lack of the proper and only motive—God alone without any other concern.

By such a confession you can be content and need not tell any other particular thing, however much it may battle against you. Receive Communion on Pentecost in addition to those days on which you usually receive.

When something distasteful or unpleasant comes your way, remember Christ crucified and be silent.

Live in faith and hope, even though you are in darkness, because it is in these darknesses that God protects the soul.

Cast your care on God, for he watches over you and will not forget you. Do not think that he leaves you alone; that would be an affront to him.

Read, pray, rejoice in God, both your good and your salvation. May he grant you this good and this salvation and conserve it all until the day of eternity. Amen. Amen. (L 20 in 1590 to a Discalced nun)

Dennis Graviss concludes that, in his letters, John consistently calls the recipient to detachment, challenges her or him to seek union, and shows his attention to the individual in his or her unique situation and journey.[9] In reference to particular letters, Graviss identifies certain consistent themes or tasks: John teaches beginners (L 2 and 12); he consoles those in darkness and difficulty (L 13, 17, 24, 28); he recognizes when to allow the Holy Spirit to work as principal director (L 7, 8, 9, 12, 13); and he answers external forum questions (L 10, 14, 18, 25).[10] These writings, together with the testimonies of those who benefited personally from his direction, make clear that he himself exemplified the qualities that he thought essential to the sound spiritual guide.

9. Graviss, *Portrait of the Spiritual Director*, 117–18.
10. Graviss, 159–60.

Chapter Eight

John of the Cross on Spiritual Direction

John of the Cross's reflections on spiritual direction focus especially on the specific qualities that he believed to be essential in a good spiritual director and that were glaring by their absence in inadequate guides. But he also offers more general insights into such topics as the importance of having a director, the necessary attitudes within the one seeking spiritual companionship, and the essential truth that God remains always the principal spiritual director. The human guide tries to help the other person to discover and to respond to the Spirit's movements, while trying to stay out of the way of the divine direction.

The Need for a Director

John of the Cross warns that it is a dangerous thing to serve as one's own guide (A 2.22.17; 2.19.7), and he insists on the importance of good spiritual guidance. He devotes at least five of his maxims in the *Sayings of Light and Love* to their necessity:

> 5. Whoever wants to stand alone without the support of a master and guide will be like the tree that stands alone in a field without a proprietor. No matter how much the tree bears, passers-by will pick the fruit before it ripens.

> 7. The virtuous soul that is alone and without a master is like a lone burning coal; it will grow colder rather than hotter.

> 8. Those who fall alone remain alone in their fall, and they value their soul little since they entrust it to themselves alone.

> 9. If you do not fear falling alone, do you presume that you will rise up alone? Consider how much more can be accomplished by two together than by one alone.

> 11. The blind person who falls will not be able to get up alone; the blind person who does get up alone will go off on the wrong road.

Recall that these little sayings were usually given individually to those seeking his guidance as a kind of particular reminder of some counsel or topic of their one-to-one discussion.

Drawing on the witness of the Bible, John notes that, especially in spiritual matters, it is always best to consult others. He points out that Moses, before setting out to lead the people of Israel out of slavery, had consulted his brother Aaron (A 2.22.10–11). In the same way, Moses accepted the counsel of his father-in-law Jethro and appointed assistants to help him with the governance of the people (A 2.22.13). John continues finding support for the importance of seeking counsel in both the Old and New Testaments:

This is why [Jesus] also affirmed in the Gospel: *Ubi fuerint duo vel tres congregati in nominee meo, ibi sum ego in medio eorum* (Where two or three are gathered to consider what is for the greater honor and glory of my name, there I am in the midst of them—that is, clarifying and confirming truths in their hearts) [Matt 18:20]. It is noteworthy that he did not say: Where there is one alone, there I am; rather, he said: Where there are at least two. Thus God announces that he does not want the soul to believe only by itself the communications it thinks are of divine origin, or for anyone to be assured or confirmed in them without the Church or her ministers. God will not bring clarification and confirmation of the truth to the heart of one who is alone. Such a person would remain weak and cold in regard to truth.

This is what Ecclesiastes extols: *Vae soli, quia cum ceciderit, non habet sublevantem se. Si dormierint duo, favebuntur mutuo: Unus quomodo calefiet? Et si quispiam praevaluerit contra unum, duo resistente ei* [Eccl 4:10-12]. This means: Woe to those who are alone, for when they fall they have no one to lift them up. If two sleep together, the one shall give warmth (the warmth of God who is in their midst) to the other; how shall one alone be warm? How shall one alone stop being cold in the things of God? . . . This is so true that even after St. Paul had been preaching the Gospel, which he heard not from humans but from God [Gal 1:12] for a long time, he could not resist going and conferring about it with St. Peter and the apostles: *ne forte in vanum currerem aut cucurrissem* (lest he should run or might have run in vain) [Gal 2:2]. He did not feel secure until he had received assurance from other people. This, then, seems remarkable, O Paul! Could not he who revealed the Gospel to you also give security from any error you might make in preaching its truth? (A 2.22.11–12)

Consultation with a spiritual guide, John observes, provides another perspective and a check offered by the reasoned consideration of another person: "God is so pleased that the rule and direction of humans be through other humans and that a person be governed by natural reason that he definitely does not want us to bestow entire credence on his supernatural communications, or be confirmed in their strength and security, until they pass through this human channel of the mouth of another human person" (A 2.22.9). John concludes that the guide and the person "come together to know the truth and practice it," and the "two together will resist the devil" (A 2.22.12). And the most fundamental truth to be sought includes, importantly, truth about oneself. John's insight into the human psyche helps him to see how deeply capable we are of self-deception, especially if we fail to take counsel from others. This is evident in his pointed, accurate, and sometimes humorous reflection on the "vices of beginners" in the *Dark Night* (N 1.2–7).

It is important to see that, for John of the Cross, spiritual direction must be understood within the context of the inherent dynamism of the maturing Christian spiritual life, its orientation toward union with God even in this life, and the presumption that the person is eagerly pursuing this path.

Such people need "suitable and alert directors who will show them the way to the summit" (A Prol.3). While John clearly recognizes that the spiritual journey is unique to each person, at the same time, there are basic, common patterns, trajectories, helps, and potential pitfalls about which an experienced, wise, and discerning director can offer helpful counsel.

While John believes that direction can be useful throughout life's journey, he obviously believes that it is his own particular contribution to focus his attention on direction at more advanced stages or seasons on that path. This is clear in his lengthiest and most focused discussion of spiritual direction in his "treatise" on the topic in the *Living Flame* (F 3.27–67). In John's experience, there were too few resources—books and human guides—to help people who want to enter more deeply into prayer and communion with God. At the end of the prologue to the *Ascent*, he notes his particular focus: "My main intention is not to address everyone, but only some of the persons of our holy order of the primitive observance of Mount Carmel, both friars and nuns, whom God favors by putting on the path leading up this mount, since they are the ones who asked me to write this work. Because they are already detached to a great extent from the temporal things of this world, they will more easily grasp this doctrine on nakedness of spirit" (A Prol.9). The prologue of the *Spiritual Canticle* tells us that it was written at the request of Mother Ana of Jesus, who, he notes, lacks academic theological training but does not lack knowledge of "mystical theology"—that is, the knowledge that comes with deep prayer (C Prol.3). The work, then, is intended especially for a reader of her mature spiritual experience.

Of particular importance to John are the transitions that can mark the deepening spiritual life—most notably, the subtle beginnings of the divine gift of contemplation. He notes the signs that the person and his or her guide should look for when God begins to introduce this gift (A 2.13.2–4; N 1.9.1–9; F 3.32). The ability to discern the invitation of the Spirit at that moment is critical, because the beginnings of contemplation, he says, are often subtle and easy to miss or misinterpret. Beyond that focus, John wants to provide assistance with working through periods of darkness and aridity and addressing the experience of special forms of divine communication and extraordinary phenomena. He devotes, for example, a chapter of the *Ascent* to the bad guidance offered by directors during these times—a chapter titled "The harm caused by some spiritual masters in not giving souls adequate guidance with regard to the visions mentioned. An explanation of how both can be misled even by visions that have a divine origin" (A 2.18). But, as we will see, bad direction was a frequent topic and deep concern for John of the Cross.

Responsibility of the Directee

But even as much as a solid guide is helpful and even necessary, people can benefit from it only if they speak with the director both clearly and honestly about what they are experiencing: "whatever is received through supernatural means (in whatever manner) should immediately be told clearly, integrally, and simply to one's spiritual master" (A 2.22.16). He urges people not simply to seek out a guide who will confirm whatever they themselves feel or judge to be the right path, who will simply think well of and admire them, or whose opinion of them is so important that they do not feel that they can be candid:

And when at times their spiritual directors, their confessors, or their superiors disapprove their spirit and method of procedure, they feel that these directors do not understand, or perhaps that this failure to approve derives from a lack of holiness, since they want these directors to regard their conduct with esteem and praise. So they quickly search for some other spiritual advisor more to their liking, someone who will congratulate them and be impressed by their deeds; and they flee, as they would death, those who attempt to place them on the safe road by forbidding these things—and sometimes they even become hostile toward such spiritual directors. . . .

Many want to be the favorites of their confessors, and thus they are consumed by a thousand envies and disquietudes. Embarrassment forbids them from relating their sins clearly, lest their reputation diminish in their confessor's eyes. They confess their sins in the most favorable light so as to appear better than they actually are, and thus they approach the confessional to excuse themselves rather than accuse themselves. Sometimes they confess the evil things they do to a different confessor so that their own confessor might think they commit no sins at all. Therefore, in their desire to appear holy, they enjoy relating their good behavior to their confessor, and in such careful terms that these good deeds appear greater than they actually are. It would be more humble of them, as we will point out later, to make light of the good they do and to wish that no one, neither their confessor nor anybody else, should consider it of any importance at all. (N 1.2.3–4)

Surely, when a person enters into a spiritual direction relationship, the guide must attend to the other person's own sense of direction and calling, but the direction relationship makes no sense if such people simply want to pursue their own path without reference to what the spiritual guide might offer by way of question or comment. Why bother with spiritual guidance if you aren't open to challenges, other ideas, or new possibilities? While we note again that John has a more "directive" sense of spiritual guidance, his basic point is not to enter into guidance if one does not want to be guided (though, as we will see, the guide too must be discerning in offering counsel and leave the person free to move as directed by the Holy Spirit):

> Some are very insistent that their spiritual director allow them to do what they themselves want to do, and finally almost force the permission from him. And if they do not get what they want, they become sad and go about like testy children. They are under the impression that they do not serve God when they are not allowed to do what they want. Since they take gratification and their own will as their support and their god, they become sad, weak, and discouraged when their director takes these from them and desires that they do God's will. They think that gratifying and satisfying themselves is serving and satisfying God. (N 1.6.3)

It is incumbent on those seeking direction to exercise caution in their choice. Entrusting themselves to another's guidance in a spirit of openness and trust must be undertaken with care since the influence of the director may be quite formative:

Let us now say something about the attitude of some confessors who give their penitents poor instructions. Assuredly, I wish I knew how to speak of this because I think it is difficult to explain how the spirit of the disciple is secretly fashioned after that of the spiritual father. This subject involves such prolixity that it is wearisome to me, for it seems one factor cannot be explained without explaining another, since in these spiritual matters things are interrelated.

But to cover the matter sufficiently here, I might point out that it seems to me—and indeed it is so—that if the spiritual father has such a bent toward revelations that they produce in his soul some effect, pleasure, or complete satisfaction, he cannot avoid—even though unaware—affecting his disciples with this attitude and pleasure if they are not more advanced than he. And even if they are more advanced, the director can do serious harm by continuing to give direction. From the inclination the spiritual father has toward these visions and the gratification he finds in them there rises a certain esteem for them, and unless he is on his guard he will manifest indications of this to the persons he is directing. And if those persons have the same inclination, there cannot be between them, as far as I can see, anything but a communication of esteem for these matters. (A 2.18.5–6)

But God Remains the Principal Director

But as important as a human spiritual director can be, John remains insistent that God always remains the principal director—"the master and guide of the soul" (N 2.16.7–8). For this reason, the person must strive to become more open, more docile, and more responsive to the movements and promptings of the Holy Spirit who acts in each person "with order, gently, and according to the mode of the soul" (A 2.17.3). "God," John remarks, "perfects people gradually, according to their human nature. . . . This is God's method to bring a soul step by step to the innermost good. . . . The process depends on what God judges expedient for the soul, or on how he wants to grant it favors" (A 2.17.4).

Because the Spirit remains the principal director, the task for a human guide is to assist in the directee's responsiveness to the Spirit and certainly not get in the way. This requires that director also be attentive, docile, and responsive to the divine action. For John, then, the guide's task is not essentially "giving direction" as such but rather helping the person to identify the obstacles within, assisting in overcoming those barriers, offering counsel to avoid common pitfalls and missteps, at times pointing at least tentatively to the Spirit's apparent movements, supporting and encouraging in periods of darkness, and, most deeply, helping the directee to rise to the true inner freedom to receive and respond to the divine self-giving.

John's focus on the true direction of the Spirit is apparent in his little "treatise" of spiritual direction in the *Living Flame*, as the following paragraphs (F 3.46–47) make evident:

> These directors should reflect that *they themselves are not the chief agent, guide, and mover of souls* in this matter, but the *principal guide is the Holy Spirit*, who is never neglectful of souls, and *they themselves are instruments* for directing these souls to perfection through faith and the law of God, *according*

to the spirit given by God to each one. Thus the whole concern of directors should not be to accommodate souls to their own method and condition, but they should observe the road along which God is leading one; if they do not recognize it, they should leave the soul alone and not bother it. *And in harmony with the path and spirit along which God leads a soul, the spiritual director should strive to conduct it into greater solitude, tranquility, and freedom of spirit.* He should give it latitude so that when God introduces it into this solitude it does not bind its corporeal or spiritual faculties to some particular object, interior or exterior, and does not become anxious or afflicted with the thought that nothing is being done. Even though the soul is not then doing anything, God is doing something in it.

Directors should strive to disencumber the soul and bring it into solitude and idleness so it may not be tied to any particular knowledge, earthly or heavenly, or to any covetousness for some satisfaction or pleasure, or to any other apprehension; and in such a way that it may be empty through the pure negation of every creature, and placed in spiritual poverty. This is what the soul must do of itself, as the Son of God counsels: *Whoever does not renounce all possessions cannot be my disciple* [emphasis in the original; Luke 14:33]. This counsel refers not only to the renunciation according to the will of all corporeal and temporal things, but also to the dispossession of spiritual things, which includes spiritual poverty, to which the Son of God ascribes beatitude [Matt 5:3].

God, like the sun, stands above souls ready to communicate himself. Let directors be content with disposing them for this according to evangelical perfection, which lies in nakedness and emptiness of sense and spirit; and let them not desire to go any further than this in building, since that function belongs only to the Father of lights from whom descends every good and perfect gift [Jas 1:17]. . . . And *since he is the supernatural artificer, he will construct supernaturally in each soul the edifice he desires, if you, director, will prepare it* by striving to annihilate it in its natural operations and affections, which have neither the ability nor strength to build the supernatural edifice. The natural operations and affections at this time impede rather than help. *It is your duty to prepare the soul, and God's office, as the Wise Man says, is to direct its path* [Prov 16:9], that is, toward supernatural goods, through modes and ways understandable to neither you nor the soul. (F 3.46–47; emphasis added)

With these general perspectives and presuppositions in mind, we can now turn our attention to John of the Cross's sometimes pointed remarks about bad directors and then to his teaching on the characteristics of good guides.

Chapter Nine

John of the Cross on Bad Directors

Much of the teaching of John of the Cross on spiritual direction comes by way of his comments on bad direction. As we have said, his writing is very much directed to those who lack direction especially in the more mature seasons of the spiritual life and to those who would be in danger of or have already experienced bad directors. He has any number of adjectives and images for such directors: "pestiferous" (*pestífera*), he calls them (F 3.62), or, in other words, pernicious or damaging. We will see a number of these images from the prologue of the *Ascent* and from the *Flame* in the paragraphs that follow: blind guides (F 3.29), like the builders of the tower of Babel (A Prol.4), like Job's comforters (A Prol.4), barriers or obstacles at the gate of heaven (F 3.62), blacksmiths who know only how to hammer (F 3.43), and foxes that destroy the flourishing vineyard (F 3.55).

In the prologue of the *Ascent* in which John is explaining his reason for writing (and in which he is offering direction in written form), he identifies a number of characteristics of an inadequate guide that will become more explicit in the *Flame*—that is, lack of knowledge, of personal experience, and of a spirit of discernment:

> *Some spiritual fathers are likely to be a hindrance and harm* rather than a help to these souls that journey on this road. Such directors *have neither understanding nor experience* of these ways. They are *like the builders of the tower of Babel* [Gen 11:1-9]. When these builders were supposed to provide the proper materials for the project, they brought entirely different supplies because *they failed to understand the language*. And thus nothing was accomplished. Hence, it is arduous and difficult for a soul in these periods of the spiritual life when it cannot understand itself or find anyone else who understands it.
>
> It will happen to individuals that while they are being conducted by God along a sublime path of dark contemplation and aridity, in which they feel lost and filled with darknesses, trials, conflicts, and temptations, they will meet someone who, *in the style of Job's comforters* [Job 4:8-11], will proclaim that all of this is due to melancholia, depression, or temperament, or to some hidden wickedness, and that as a result God has forsaken them. Therefore the usual verdict is that these individuals must have lived an evil life since such trials afflict them.
>
> Other directors will tell them that they are falling back since they find no satisfaction or consolation as they previously did in the things of God. Such talk only doubles the trial of a poor soul. It will happen that the soul's greatest suffering will be caused by the knowledge of its own miseries. That it is full of evil and sin is as clear as day to it, and even clearer, for, as we shall say further on, God is the author of this enlightenment in the night of contemplation. And when this

soul finds someone who agrees with what it feels (that these trials are all its own fault), its suffering and distress grow without bounds. And this suffering usually becomes worse than death. Such a confessor is not satisfied with this but, in judging these trials to be the result of sin, he urges souls who endure them to go over their past and make many general confessions—which is another crucifixion. *The director does not understand* that now perhaps is not the time for such activity. Indeed, it is a period for leaving these persons alone in the purgation God is working in them, a time to give comfort and encouragement that they may desire to endure this suffering as long as God wills, for until then no remedy—whatever the soul does, or the confessor says—is adequate.

With divine help we will discuss all this: how individuals should behave; what method the confessor should use in dealing with them; signs to recognize this purification of the soul that we call the dark night; whether it is the purification of the senses or of the spirit; and how we can discern whether this affliction is caused by melancholia or some other deficiency of sense or spirit.

Some souls—or their confessors—may think that God is leading them along this road of the dark night of spiritual purgation, but perhaps this will not be so. What they suffer will be due to one of these deficiencies. Likewise, many individuals think they are not praying when, indeed, their prayer is deep. Others place high value on their prayer while it amounts to little more than nothing. (A Prol.4–6; emphasis added)

But it is in his lengthy discussion of spiritual guides in the commentary on the third stanza of the *Living Flame of Love* (F 3.29–67) that John of the Cross gives his lengthiest and most detailed critique of bad direction—often related especially to failure to know the signs of the introduction of contemplation, since these movements can be subtle and delicate (see F 3.43). Here, the overriding image for inadequate directors is "blind guides" (in contrast to God who is the principal and true guide). The human director is, in fact, just one of three possible inadequate guides: the spiritual director, the devil, and the unguided person himself or herself:

> The soul, then, should advert that God is the principal agent in this matter. He acts as guide of the blind, leading it by the hand to the place it knows not how to reach (to supernatural things of which neither its intellect nor will nor memory can know the nature). It should use all its principal care in watching so as not to place any obstacle in the way of God, its guide on this road ordained for it by him according to the perfection of his law and of the faith, as we said.
>
> It can cause this obstacle by allowing itself to be led by another blind guide. There are three blind guides who can draw it off the road: the spiritual director, the devil, and the soul itself. So the soul may understand how this happens, we will briefly discuss each of these blind guides. (F 3.29)

Although he mentions all three blind guides, his principal concern is evident in the fact that, in the paragraphs that follow, he spends three paragraphs on the devil as a blind guide (F 3.63–65), two on the person as his or her own blind guide (F 3.66–67), but thirty-three on the bad director as a blind guide (F 3.30–62)![1]

1. Thomas H. Green, *The Friend of the Bridegroom: Spiritual Direction and the Encounter with Christ* (Notre Dame, IN: Ave Maria Press, 2000), 82.

In the course of these paragraphs of the *Living Flame*, John identifies three main characteristics or faults of these bad directors: (1) they lack a depth of personal spiritual experience and knowledge and thus cannot guide a soul beyond the beginnings; (2) they lack adequate sensitivity and discernment of the movements of the Spirit, and so they fail to offer counsel in keeping with the individual person's present place on the journey; and (3) they are possessive and jealous, and so constrict rather than promote the freedom of the ones whom they guide and thus show their underlying worldly values.

(1) *Lack of experience*: For John, the lack of experience is most evident in the failure to know how to respond when the directee is beginning to experience the gift of contemplative prayer. The inexperienced director—"inexperienced" not so much in the ministry of direction as in the depth of his or her own personal spiritual maturity—does not know the signs that include especially a distinctive experience of dryness or aridity in prayer. The guide continues to direct the person back to active forms of meditation when, in fact, the Spirit is inviting him or her into a deeper, wordless prayer. John believes that God calls many to contemplation. But in its early stages, it is difficult to discern, leading too many to turn away. John, therefore, has a harsh judgment for spiritual guides who, lacking the necessary personal spiritual experience and depth of knowledge in order to assist the person at this critical period, give bad direction. His assessment, as we read below, is that "these directors do not know what spirit is"!

> These spiritual masters, not understanding souls that tread the path of quiet and solitary contemplation, since they themselves

have not reached it and do not know what it is to part with discursive meditation, think these souls are idle. They hinder them and hamper the peace of restful and quiet contemplation that God of his own was according them, by making them walk along the path of meditation and imaginative reflection, and perform interior acts. In doing this, these souls find great repugnance, dryness, and distraction; they want to remain in their holy idleness and quiet and peaceful recollection.

Since the senses find nothing to be attached to, take pleasure in, or do in this recollection, these directors also persuade souls to strive for satisfaction and feelings of fervor when they should be counseling the opposite. When these persons cannot accomplish this as before, because the time for such activity has passed and this is not their road, they grow doubly disquieted, thinking that they are lost. Their directors foster this belief in them, cause in them aridity of spirit, and deprive them of the precious anointings God was bestowing on them in solitude and tranquility. This causes serious harm, as I said; and these directors bring them grief and ruin, for on the one hand such persons lose ground, and on the other they suffer a useless affliction.

These directors do not know what spirit is [emphasis added]. They do a great injury to God and show disrespect toward him by intruding with a rough hand where he is working. It cost God a great deal to bring these souls to this stage, and he highly values his work of having introduced them into this solitude and emptiness regarding their faculties and activity so that he might speak to their hearts, which is what he always desires. Since it is he who now reigns in the soul with an abundance of peace and calm, he takes the initiative himself by making the natural acts of the faculties fail, by which the soul laboring the whole night accomplished nothing [Luke

5:5]; and he feeds the spirit without the activity of the senses because neither the sense nor its function is capable of spirit.

The extent to which God values this tranquility and sleep, or annihilation of sense, is clear in the entreaty, so notable and efficacious, that he made in the Song of Songs: *I adjure you, daughters of Jerusalem, by the roes and the harts of the fields, that you stir not up nor awaken my beloved until she please* [Song 3:5]. He hereby indicates how much he loves solitary sleep and forgetfulness, for he compares it to these animals that are so retiring and withdrawn. Yet these spiritual directors do not want the soul to rest and remain quiet, but want it always to labor and work, so that consequently it does not allow room for God's work and through its own activity ruins and effaces what he is doing. Its activities are like the little foxes that destroy the flourishing vineyard of the soul [Song 2:15]. Thus the Lord complains through Isaiah: *You have devoured my vineyard* [Isa 3:14]. (F 3.53–55)

In fact, John views such failure by a director, even if done with a sincere but misguided ignorance, as a serious thwarting of God's desire and will for the person. In John's mind, it risks serious judgment from God:

Perhaps in their zeal these directors err with good will because they do not know any better. Not for this reason, however, should they be excused for the counsels they give rashly, without first understanding the road and spirit a person may be following, and for rudely meddling in something they do not understand, instead of leaving the matter to one who does understand. It is no light matter or fault to cause a soul to lose inestimable goods and sometimes leave it in ruin through temerarious counsel.

Thus one who recklessly errs will not escape a punishment corresponding to the harm caused, for such a one is obliged to be certain, as is everyone in the performance of duties. The affairs of God must be handled with great tact and open eyes, especially in so vital and sublime a matter as is that of these souls, where there is at stake almost an infinite gain in being right and almost an infinite loss in being wrong. (F 3.56)

(2) *Lack of discernment*: The inadequate guide lacks the necessary discernment and prudence to recognize the movements of the Spirit and to appreciate the needs of the person as a unique individual at a particular moment. Too often, such guides are trying to fit the person into their own personal framework rather than discern the actual needs of the person and the divine promptings in a particular moment. When the delicate touch of a true artist is needed to help a person to discern the subtle but sublime artistry of the Spirit at work within the soul, the undiscerning guide will mar "the delicate painting" with a "coarse hand." It is in reference to this defect that John uses the image of an inexperienced blacksmith:

How often is God anointing a contemplative soul with some very delicate unguent of loving knowledge, serene, peaceful, solitary, and far withdrawn from the senses and what is imaginable, as a result of which it cannot meditate or reflect on anything, or enjoy anything heavenly or earthly (since God has engaged it in that lonely idleness and given it the inclination to solitude), when a spiritual director will happen along who, like a blacksmith, knows no more than how to hammer and pound with the faculties. Since hammering with the faculties is this director's only teaching, and he knows no more than how to meditate, he will say: "Come, now, lay aside these rest periods, which amount to idleness and a waste of time; take and meditate and make interior acts, for it is necessary that you do your part; this other method is the way of illusions and typical of fools." (F 3.43)

In a later paragraph, John uses the image of woodcarvers who must know which skills are called for at different points of the work and recognize their own limitations to perform all of the necessary functions:

Not everyone capable of hewing the wood knows how to carve the statue, nor does everyone able to carve know how to perfect and polish the work, nor do all who know how to polish it know how to paint it, nor do all who can paint it know how to put the finishing touches on it and bring the work to completion. One can do with the statue only what one knows how to do, and when craftsmen try to do more than they know how to do, the statue is ruined.

Let us see, then: If you are only a hewer, which lies in guiding the soul to contempt of the world and mortification of its appetites, or a good carver, which consists in introducing it to holy meditations, and know no more, how can you lead this soul to the ultimate perfection of delicate painting, which no longer requires hewing or carving or even relief work, but the work that God must do in it?

It is certain that if you always bind it to your teaching, which is ever of one kind, it will either backslide or fail to advance. What, I ask, will the statue look like if all you do is hammer and hew, which, in the case of the soul, is the active use of the faculties? When will the statue be complete? When or how will it be left for God to paint? Is it possible that all these functions are yours and that you are so perfect the soul will never need any other than you? (F 3.57–58)

(3) *Possessiveness and jealousy, revealing a worldly spirit*: A third characteristic of a bad director is possessiveness or jealousy when a directee consults others or when it becomes clear that he or she would benefit from the guidance of another person. Rather than support the person's freedom and thus his or her authentic growth according to the guidance of the Spirit, the bad director becomes jealous and takes personally the other person's desire to seek a new guide. John continues from the section quoted above:

Granted that you may possess the requisites for the full direction of some soul (for perhaps it does not have the talent to make progress), it is impossible for you to have the qualities demanded for the guidance of all those you refuse to allow out of your hands. God leads each one along different paths so that hardly one spirit will be found like another in even half its method of procedure. For who is there who would become, like St. Paul, all things to all so as to win them all [1 Cor 9:22]? You tyrannize souls and deprive them of their freedom, and judge for yourself the breadth of the evangelical doctrine. Therefore you endeavor to hold on to your penitents. But what is worse, you may by chance learn that one of them has consulted another (for perhaps you were not the suitable one to consult, or that person was led by God to another so as to learn what you did not teach), and you treat that peni-

tent—I am ashamed to say it—with the very jealous quar-
relsomeness we find among married couples. And this is not
jealousy for the glory of God, but a jealousy motivated by your
own pride and presumption or some other imperfection, for
you should not assume that in turning from you this person
turned from God.

God becomes extremely indignant with such directors and
in Ezekiel promises them chastisement: *You ate the milk of my
flock and you covered yourself with their wool and did not feed my
flock; I will seek my flock at your hand*, he says [Ezek 34:3, 10].

Spiritual masters, then, should give freedom to souls and
encourage them in their desire to seek improvement. The
director does not know the means by which God may wish
to benefit a soul, especially if it is no longer satisfied with the
director's teaching. This dissatisfaction is in fact a sign that
the director is not helping it, either because God is making it
advance by a road different from the one along which it is
being led, or because the master has changed style. These
masters should themselves counsel this change; all the rest
stems from foolish pride and presumption, or some other
ambition. (F 3.59–61)

Freedom is central for John of the Cross. Each of us must
strive for a deeper and more authentic freedom to respond to
God. And it is the task of the director to aid in the development of this fundamental inner liberty—not hinder it by possessiveness, jealousy, and ignorance, which is itself the result
of a lack of the necessary experience and learning. In this, the
spiritual guide must be like Moses who led the people of Israel
out of slavery into a greater freedom: "O spiritual master, guide

it to the land of promise flowing with milk and honey [Exod 3:8, 17]. Behold that for this holy liberty and idleness of the children of God, God calls the soul to the desert" (F 3.38).

John then goes on, apparently continuing his thought on possessive and jealous guides, suggesting that those vices are joined with a deeper worldliness on the part of the director:

> Let us . . . speak of another more pestiferous trait of these directors or of other worse methods used by them. It will happen that God is anointing some souls with the unctions of holy desires and motives for renouncing the world, changing their way of life, and serving him, with contempt of the world (and God esteems this stage to which he has brought them, because worldly things do not please him), when these directors, by their human rationalizations or reflections singularly contrary to the doctrine of Christ and of his humility and contempt for all things, and by depending on their own interests or satisfactions, or out of fear where there is no reason to fear, either make matters difficult for these souls or cause them to delay, or even worse try to make them put the thought from their minds. With a spirit not too devout, with little of Christ's meekness, and fully clothed in worldliness, since they do not enter by the narrow gate of life, these directors do not let others enter either.
>
> Our Lord threatens them through St. Luke: *Woe to you, for you have taken away the key of knowledge, and you neither enter yourselves nor do you allow others to enter* [Luke 11:52].
>
> These directors are indeed like barriers or obstacles at the gate of heaven, hindering those who seek their counsel from entering. They know that God has commanded them not only

to allow and help souls enter but even to compel them to enter, when he says through St. Luke: *Make them enter that my house may be filled with guests* [Luke 14:23]. But they, on the contrary, compel them to stay out. (F 3.62)

John's sometimes harsh condemnation of inadequate guides manifests a deeper sense that the work of accompanying others along the spiritual path is a serious responsibility, since it involves cooperating with—or, sadly, opposing or hindering—God's desire and action for the good of the person accompanied. He summarizes the section on bad human directors with a dire warning:

The director is thus a blind guide who can be an obstacle to the life of the soul, which is the Holy Spirit. We discover this to be the case with spiritual masters in the many ways we mentioned, in which some are aware of it and others are unaware. But neither will escape punishment; since this is their duty, they are obliged to be careful and understand what they are doing. (F 3.62)

And the possible missteps and misdirection that can result from having chosen an inadequate guide leads John to urge great care in choosing a director, because "the spirit of the disciple is secretly fashioned after that of the spiritual father" (A 2.18.6).

Chapter Ten

John of the Cross on Good Directors

Having outlined John of the Cross's reflections on misguided guidance, we have, by a kind of *via negativa*, already largely come to see how he understands the nature of good direction and especially the qualities that a solid guide should possess. But an explicit and more positive statement of these qualities will make clearer his teaching on the matter. At the very beginning of the *Ascent* (Prol.3-4), John offers some general terms to describe these necessary characteristics: the director must be "suitable and awake" (*idóneas y despierto*) and must possess "light (wisdom) and experience" (*luz y experiencia*). But, over the course of his writings, it becomes clear, as Dennis Graviss concludes, that the primary qualities of the director, for John, are three: experience, wisdom (knowledge), and discretion.[1] They are, Graviss judges, distinguishable but

1. Dennis Graviss, *Portrait of the Spiritual Director in the Writings of Saint John of the Cross*, 2nd ed. (Rome, Italy: Edizioni Carmelitane, 2014), 10.

interrelated, and all of them are necessary.[2] John of the Cross makes these three characteristics explicit when he writes:

> Let them realize that for this journey, especially its most sublime parts (and even for the intermediate parts), they will hardly find a guide accomplished as to all their needs, for besides being learned and discreet, a director should have experience. Although the foundation for guiding a soul to spirit is knowledge and discretion, directors will not succeed in leading the soul onward in it when God bestows it, nor will they even understand it if they have no experience of what true and pure spirit is. (F 3.30)

Experience

In the previous discussion of bad directors, we saw that the type of experience with which John is most concerned is not necessarily experience in offering spiritual guidance, though we can assume that, over time, a director will mature in knowledge and skills in assisting different persons in different moments of their lives and spiritual journeys. We recall that at least two of Teresa's earliest Jesuit directors were quite young and only recently ordained—and, in that culture, unlikely to have offered direction before ordination. John himself was still fairly young when he became confessor at the Monastery of the Incarnation and director to Teresa. With regard to experience as a quality of those offering spiritual guidance,

2. Graviss, 207–8.

John—again, like Teresa—is more concerned about the director's personal experience in the spiritual path. Today, we would see that this involves a personal commitment to the life of prayer and ongoing conversion. The guide must be mature in the spiritual life, in the sense of having walked the path and thus able to recognize helpful directions and possible pitfalls. The good spiritual guide must have personal experience in the ways of the Spirit and grown accustomed to listening to the Spirit's voice.[3]

Experience, of course, is necessarily linked with the other two qualities. The director's own experience is not necessarily the same as that of the one being guided. God is sometimes a God of surprises, so the guide's own familiarity with the Spirit's movement in his or her own life does not necessarily equate to expertise in pointing definitively to the divine call in another. The guide's experience is aided by the gift and skill of discernment—both being able to assist another in discerning the movement of the Spirit as well as discerning about whether and how one's own experience might be useful in guiding other people where they find themselves. Knowledge of the spiritual tradition likewise keeps directors from placing too much credence in their own subjective experience, unchecked by the experience and insights of the ages. The spiritual guide's experience, moreover, must be reflected-on experience—that is, involve a good measure of critical and

3. Graviss, 208–10; Joel Giallanza, "Spiritual Direction According to St. John of the Cross," in *Spiritual Direction: Contemporary Readings*, ed. Kevin Culligan (Locust Valley, NY: Living Flame Press, 1983), 197–99.

self-critical reflection on raw experience in light of the Christian faith and its resources.

As we have seen above, John is especially concerned that the spiritual guide be able to help the person to discern the transitional moments in the spiritual life. And of particular importance is the sometimes subtle introduction of the divine gift of contemplation.[4] For John, this involves especially an ability to understand the experience of dryness or aridity as well as its various possible origins in the life and prayer of the directee. While John himself offers three signs of this key transition in the spiritual life (A 2.13.2–4; N 1.9.1–9; F 3.32), the director must have weathered the trials and challenges of the aridity that is inevitable in the spiritual life and formed some ability to discern its roots in our own actions and in God's. It is the absence of such experience (and knowledge and discernment) that is at the heart of some of John's harshest criticisms of bad directors.

---

4. Graviss (*Portrait of the Spiritual Director*, 115–16) raises the important question whether John of the Cross believed that spiritual guides must themselves be contemplatives and mystics in order to direct contemplatives and mystics. John does not explicitly say so, though his comments on direction might seem to suggest it. Graviss concludes that, for John, the presence of the other two qualities—knowledge and discernment—would probably suffice, especially when another director is not available. Spiritual guides must know their own limitations and proceed with humility. This conclusion is consistent with what Teresa of Jesus says more explicitly about turning to a director with knowledge and discernment when one with contemplative and mystical experience is lacking.

In the *Ascent*, John speaks briefly about the importance of the spiritual life of the preacher in order to preach effectively. Skill and experience cannot replace the essential element of the quality of the preacher's interior life. The mission, essential qualities, and fundamental skills of good preachers and sound spiritual guides are not necessarily the same. But, in light of what we have said thus far about John's teaching on the qualities of a good spiritual guide, it is not difficult to apply to directors the same challenge he offers to preachers:

> As for the preacher, in order to benefit the people and avoid the impediment of vain joy and presumption, he should keep in mind that preaching is more a spiritual practice than a vocal one. For although it is practiced through exterior words, it has no force or efficacy save from the interior spirit. No matter how lofty the doctrine preached, or polished the rhetoric, or sublime the style in which the preaching is clothed, the profit does not ordinarily increase because of these means in themselves; it comes from the spirit. God's word is indeed efficacious of itself according to David, who says that *God will give to his voice the voice of power* [Ps 68:33]; yet fire also has power to burn but will not burn if the material is unprepared. . . .
>
> We frequently see, insofar as it is possible to judge here below, that the better the life of the preacher the more abundant the fruit, no matter how lowly his style, poor his rhetoric, and plain the doctrine. For the living spirit enkindles fire. But when this spirit is wanting the gain is small, however sublime the style and doctrine. Although it is true that good style, gestures, sublime doctrine, and well-chosen words are more moving and productive of effect when accompanied by this good spirit, yet without it the sermon imparts little or no

devotion to the will even though it may be delightful and pleasing to the senses and the intellect. (A 3.45.2, 4)

Knowledge/Wisdom

John of the Cross shares with Teresa of Jesus the concern that a good director must have knowledge of Scripture and the Church's teachings. But perhaps because he himself had a formal theological education, he seems more to presume than discuss academic learning as an essential quality for a sound spiritual guide. He himself turns to such formal learning as protection against error in his own writing. He begins the *Ascent*, for example, with the statement:

> In discussing this dark night, therefore, I will not rely on ex-
> perience or science, for these can fail and deceive us. Although
> I will not neglect whatever possible use I can make of them,
> my help in all that, with God's favor, I shall say, will be Sacred
> Scripture, at least in the most important matters, or those that
> are difficult to understand. Taking Scripture as our guide we
> do not err, since the Holy Spirit speaks to us through it. Should
> I misunderstand or be mistaken on some point, whether I
> deduce it from Scripture or not, I will not be intending to devi-
> ate from the true meaning of Sacred Scripture or from the
> doctrine of our Holy Mother the Catholic Church. Should
> there be some mistake, I submit entirely to the Church, or even
> to anyone who judges more competently about the matter than
> I. (A Prol.2)

But without denying the essential knowledge that comes from reading and study, John also has in mind a kind of knowledge that is more tied to experience—a kind of intuitive knowledge of the ways of God and of human nature. Graviss points out how, in Spanish, John uses two different words that can be translated into English as "knowledge." *Ciencia* is the kind of knowledge that comes from academic learning, but *saber* refers to a knowledge that comes from experience and discernment. And the verb *saber* is related to the Spanish word *sabor*, which refers to taste or flavor. Even so, *saber* refers to a kind of knowing that "tastes" the truth. In Latin, as Graviss goes on to point out, we might say that a mystic has *sapida sapientia* ("savory wisdom" or "flavorful knowledge").[5]

In this light, Graviss notes John's obvious affinity for the Bible's Wisdom books.[6] References to God's wisdom (*sabiduría*) appear more than fifty times in his works. In the Catholic tradition, wisdom is one of the gifts of the Holy Spirit that enables a person to know more deeply the things of God and to see normal realities in light of eternity. It is an attribute of God that can be given to human beings, and Graviss argues that this sense of the gift of wisdom marks John's admonition to seek spiritual guides who possess such a divinely gifted manner of knowing. Such knowing is not contrary to what can be acquired through learning or experience but rather enlightens it. The wise spiritual guide, then, is especially suited to guiding a person in the ways and will of God—provided that this spiritual companion embraces and nurtures that divine gift in prayer and matures it through practice.

5. Graviss, 130.
6. Graviss, 135–37.

Of special concern is the need for the director to have a solid knowledge of the general progression of maturing prayer from being predominantly our work of saying prayers and actively meditating on the Scriptures and mysteries of the faith to a quieter and more receptive stature, preparing for the divine gift of contemplation.

> *Thus, not understanding the stages of prayer or the ways of the spirit* [emphasis added], these directors are not aware that those acts they say the soul should make, and the discursive reflection they want it to practice, have already been accomplished. The soul has already reached the negation and silence of the senses and of meditation, and has come to the way of the spirit that is contemplation. In contemplation the activity of the senses and of discursive reflection terminates, and God alone is the agent who then speaks secretly to the solitary and silent soul. These directors fail to observe that if they want to make souls who in this fashion have attained to spirit still walk the path of the senses, they will cause them to turn back and become distracted. If those who have reached the end of their journey continue to walk in order to reach the end, they will necessarily move away from that end, besides doing something ridiculous. Once individuals, through the activity of their faculties, have reached the quiet recollection that every spiritual person pursues, in which the functioning of these faculties ceases, it would not merely be useless for them to repeat the acts of these same faculties in order to reach this recollection, but it would be harmful, for in abandoning the recollection already possessed they would become distracted. (F 3.44)

In the end, it becomes apparent that, for John of the Cross, the sound spiritual guide must have studied and reflected on, in a prayerful way, the Sacred Scriptures. He or she must have a good knowledge of the spiritual wisdom of the past that comes from the long history of Christian spirituality.[7] We know that, in this tradition, there have been many voices, each with its own emphases and insights, addressing different needs in different times. In order to meet the individuality of persons in direction, the spiritual guide must be able to draw reliably on insights from this spiritual and theological heritage. But, more deeply, as Graviss notes, the "wisdom" of the director must come from a sharing in the divine wisdom itself, encountered in the spiritual guide's own deepening relationship with God and prayer.[8]

Discretion

John of the Cross was a person madly in love with God, as is clearly revealed in his poetry. He was a founding member of the male branch of the Discalced reform. And in its early years zealous young friars and nuns were joining the reform precisely for its spiritual fervor and rigor. His writing was directed primarily at these religious and their lay associates. What we today might read as austere and demanding was, to his first readers, the spirit with which they themselves burned. His famous (or, for some, perhaps his infamous) *nada* doctrine—summarized early in the *Ascent* (A 1.13)—must be understood as the passion

7. Graviss, 208–10.
8. Graviss, 161–62.

to leave aside anything that might separate him from his Be-loved (a sentiment familiar to secular love poems and songs in which a lover professes a willingness to "climb any mountain," etc.). At the same time, even at his most rigorous, John notes that this spiritual teaching must be "put into practice with order and discretion" (A 1.13.7). In the *Dark Night*, which is essen-tially a second volume to the *Ascent*, he calls excessive bodily penances, pursued without discretion and without consultation with a spiritual guide, "no more than the penance of beasts" (N 1.6.2). Such ascetical practices serve to promote vice rather than virtue. This spirit of discretion or prudence is obvious in his extant letters (if not always so apparent in some sections of his commentaries when read in isolation).

The truth is that Teresa found the young John of the Cross to be a bit too rigorous. While she reports that she was im-pressed and edified by the earnest asceticism of the first foun-dation of men at Duruelo, she counselled a greater moderation (F 14.12). Apparently, John embraced her moderating counsel sufficiently so that, not too long after, he was sent to the Dis-calced friars' first novitiate in Pastrana to bring moderation to the excessive rigors of its novice master. By the time that Teresa arranged for him to join her as the confessor at the Calced Monastery of the Incarnation in 1572, where she had been ordered to go as prioress, his prudence had reached its maturity. As we have noted, although the Calced nuns there initially feared John's reputation for austerity and asceticism, they were quickly won over by his gentleness and skill in guiding them, which he provided without trying to bring them to embrace the greater asceticism of the Discalced reform. Such prudent discretion is in keeping with the admonition of the "primitive rule" of St. Albert of Jerusalem—the foundational Carmelite document, for both Calced and Discalced—which, after urging zeal in the Carmelite vocation, teaches: "See that the bonds of common sense are not exceeded, however, for common sense is the guide of the virtues."[9]

In speaking of this third essential quality of spiritual directors, John uses a number of different but related terms: *discreto* (discreet),[10] *discretamente* (discreetly),[11] *discreción* (discretion),[12] *discreción de espíritus* (discernment of spirits),[13] and *prudencia* and *prudente* (prudence/prudent).[14] Together, they describe a good director as humanly prudent, moderate, able to "size up" persons and situations, having sound intuition and solid good judgment, and possessing the mature spiritual gift of discerning the movement of the Spirit in the directee but also in the director's own heart.[15] For John of the Cross, the word "discretion" (in its various forms) as an attribute of the good director, then, is synonymous with both discernment of spirits and prudence.[16]

---

9. Quoted by Kevin Culligan, "Toward a Model of Spiritual Direction Based on the Writings of Saint John of the Cross and Carl Rogers: An Exploratory Study" (PhD diss., Boston University Graduate School, 1979), 44n1.

10. A 2.28.1; 3.30.5; F 3.30.

11. A 1.13.7; C 2.8.

12. SLL Prol; A 2.18.2; 3.21.1; N 1.6.1–2; F 3.29; LE 12.

13. A 2.26.11; 3.30.1.

14. A 2.19.14; 2.26.13; 3.13.9; 3.23.3; 3.29.4.

15. See Graviss, *Portrait of the Spiritual Director*, 181.

16. Aniano Álvarez-Suárez, "Dirección espiritual," in *Diccionario de San Juan de la Cruz*, ed. Eulogio Pacho (Burgos, Spain: Editorial Monte Carmelo, 2009), 341.

The director must be able to attend to the individual person before him or her, discerning their situation at the moment, the state of their readiness to move along, and an appropriate response that would prove helpful at a particular moment for a particular person. Whatever learning or knowledge the director possesses is useful to this particular directee only if he or she can discern how and when it might prove useful.[17] While John himself conveys an urgency to move along the path, he is aware that the director must be able to be gentle and supportive when it would be the most useful attitude toward the directee:

> It ought to be noted in this regard that, even though we have greatly stressed rejection of these [mystical] communications and the duty of confessors to forbid souls from making them a topic of conversation, *spiritual fathers should not show severity, displeasure, or scorn* in dealing with these souls. With such an attitude they would make them cower and shrink from a manifestation of these experiences, would close the door to these souls, and cause them many difficulties. Since God is leading them by this means, there is no reason to oppose it or become frightened or scandalized over it. *The spiritual father should instead proceed with much kindness and calm. He should give these souls encouragement and the opportunity to speak about their experiences*, and, if necessary, oblige them to do so, for at times everything is needful on account of the hardship some find in discussing these matters. (A 2.22.19; emphasis added)

17. Graviss, *Portrait of the Spiritual Director*, 208–10.

In the *Dark Night* (N 1.1–7), John of the Cross manifests his gift as a kind of spiritual psychologist in offering a wonderfully insightful reflection on the "vices of beginners" (though in that context "beginners" means beginners in the contemplative way). There he offers a distinctive and more spiritual interpretation of the traditional capital sins (that is, pride, avarice, lust, envy, gluttony, anger, and sloth). Each is understood as a different way in which people can become self-deceived and thus hinder their own growth in openness to the grace that makes contemplation possible. It is the quality of discretion that would allow a good director to recognize the manifestations of these vices in a directee and to discern if, when, and how a challenge toward greater self-awareness might be appropriate. Fundamentally, of course, the goal is to help the directee to grow in their own critical self-knowledge and discernment.

It is perhaps in book 2 of the *Ascent*—in which he is addressing the discerning of spiritual experiences and divine communications—that John offers his most pointed indications of the need for discretion in the spiritual guide.[18] As is often the case, John speaks of the essential quality by looking at the effect of its absence in a director:

> The reason motivating me to enlarge somewhat on this subject is the want of discretion that I have noticed—from what I can understand—in some spiritual masters. Trusting these supernatural apprehensions, counting them to be authentic

18. Graviss, 181.

and of divine origin, these directors together with their penitents have gone astray and become bewildered, realizing in themselves the words of our Savior: *Si caecus caeco ducatum praestet, ambo in foveam cadunt* (If one blind person leads another, both fall into the pit) [Matt 15:14]. He does not say they will fall, but that they do fall. It is not necessary to wait until they fall into error in order for them to fall. The mere fact that the one blind person dares to be guided by the other is already an error; and thus the first, though less serious, fall is taken. (A 2.18.2)

Later in the *Ascent*, he suggests that discernment in the director is particularly a spiritual gift:

It is worthy of note, though, that individuals whose spirit is purified can naturally perceive—some more than others—the inclinations and talents of other persons and what lies in the heart or interior spirit. They derive this knowledge through exterior indications (even though extremely slight) such as words, gestures, and other signs. Just as the devil, because he is a spirit, is endowed with this skill, so is the spiritual person, according to the Apostle: *Spiritualis autem judicat omnia* (The spiritual person judges all things) [1 Cor 2:15]. And again he declares: *Spiritus enim omnia scrutatur, etiam profunda Dei* (The spirit searches all things, even the deep things of God) [1 Cor 2:10]. Although spiritual persons cannot know naturally the thoughts of others or their interior state, they can know this clearly through supernatural enlightenment or through exterior indications. And though they can often be deceived in the knowledge deduced from these indications, they are more often correct in their surmise. [John concludes, though, that directors must not put excessive trust in this type of knowl-edge.] (A 2.26.14)

John is interested in helping and really urging people and their directors to promote the wholehearted pursuit of holi-ness and union with God—to the degree that it is in their power, with the help of grace. But even with this exalted goal in mind, the discerning guide must know when the task of the moment is to try to gently nudge a person along, challenge, or simply offer encouragement. Speaking of moments of un-avoidable dryness along the way, John urges the director: "In-deed, it is a period for leaving these persons alone in the purgation God is working in them, a time to give comfort and encouragement that they may desire to endure this suffering as long as God wills, for until then no remedy—whatever the soul does or the confessor says—is adequate" (A Prol.5).

The quality of discretion in a spiritual guide involves both the ability to be discerning about the situation and movement of the Spirit in the directee but also in one's self. The discerning guide must be able to recognize when he or she is no longer the best companion as the other person's journey takes a new direction or step. This is a discernment both of the director's own skills and limits as well as the subtle developments in the life and prayer of the other. In the spiritual guide, this requires both discernment and the inner freedom to let a directee go without attachment, possessiveness, jealousy, or false pride—and to recognize such stirrings in him- or herself.

It must be the director's goal to promote freedom in the directee, and this requires that he or she have the inner freedom to let go willingly. As we mentioned in speaking of bad directors, the guide must be like Moses, John says, leading the directee into freedom: "O spiritual master, guide it to the land of promise flowing with milk and honey" (F 3.38). It is, after all, as we have seen, the Holy Spirit who is the true and ultimate guide of the person. It is the task of the director to assist the Spirit as he or she is able but otherwise to stay out of the way. The relationship is principally for the good of the directee, not the director.

A special challenge for a spiritual director is the ability to distinguish melancholy or depression from spiritual aridity/dryness. (We saw that this was also a concern for Teresa of Jesus.) For John of the Cross, aridity is one of the signs for discerning the subtle divine invitation to true contemplation (see A 2.13.6; N 1.9.2–3). In fact, the experience of dryness in prayer can arise from a number of different sources, including what we today would identify as depression or the growth of half-heartedness or carelessness in prayer.

Conclusion

Speaking of both bad and good directors, John of the Cross identifies broadly the same qualities that Teresa of Jesus views as essential. The director must be experienced in the sense of mature in a personal relationship with Christ, knowing through his or her own journey some of the possible ups and downs, pitfalls, and helps to authentic Christian development. Of special value, especially in order to guide persons more advanced in prayer, is personal experience of a deeper encounter with God in prayer. Together with the first, the second quality is knowledge, both in the sense of study of Scripture and spirituality as well as the wise, more intuitive knowledge that comes with mature spiritual experience. The third characteristic, intertwined with the others, is a spirit of discernment, in the sense of discerning the movement of the Spirit both in self and in the other and also in the actual place in which the other finds himself or herself.

Conclusion

Insights for Today

Teresa of Avila and John of the Cross share a dynamic view of the Christian life. We are on a journey, ascending Mount Carmel (according to the image of one of John's principal works), following a way that leads to our fullest and most authentic fulfillment (according to the image of Teresa's *Way of Perfection*), or walking on a path through interior dwelling places that lead to union with the God who dwells in the center of every human soul (the defining image of her *Interior Castle*). Both of them, like their first readers, were zealous in seeking to progress along this path. They held out hope that God wills divine union for us even in this life. And so, they viewed the role of the spiritual director to be of assistance to—and in that sense, to walk with or to companion—those who had been awakened to God's call and self-offer. But it always remains a goal offered by God, made possible by God, directed for each individual according to the divine plan. The human guide must attempt to be an instrument in helping the person to be guided, directed, and empowered by God.

As we have mentioned throughout the book, Teresa and John wrote in a different age and culture. And this inevitably colored their perspective and emphases. We have seen why, for example, their sense of the role of a spiritual director is often more explicitly directive than contemporary models would recommend—though they too remained utterly emphatic that the Spirit remains the principal and true director. In the same way, with an eye to their own distinctive world, their view tends to be more pedagogical—more about teaching—than contemporary writers would suggest. But, for Teresa and John, the teaching or instruction that was offered was intended to suggest not a one-size-fits-all plan but rather a way of offering insights and cautions drawn from the long Christian tradition and seeking to keep sincere persons from straying beyond the boundaries offered by Sacred Scripture.

To some degree, as a reflection of their spiritual culture, Teresa and especially John focus on the ascetical aspects of the Christian journey that make the docile reception of the gift of contemplation possible. And the usually gentle proddings and encouragement by a director can be of great assistance in this undertaking. We must rid ourselves (i.e., John's emphasis on purgation) of obstacles to discerning and responding to God's action, invitation, and self-gift. We must be made free, by our own graced efforts but ultimately and more deeply by contemplative receptivity to God's purifying action. Asceticism certainly receives much less attention and emphasis in our day, and it is a positive contemporary development not to focus excessive attention on sin and guilt. But sin is a fact of human existence in every age, and it is a hindrance to deeper communion with God—at first and especially mortal sin but, with the deepening of the Christian life and prayer, so too with venial sin. Proponents of contemporary contemplative practice rightly emphasize the cleansing and healing effects of deepening prayer itself—and Teresa was utterly consistent in pointing to the fruits of increased virtue and inner freedom that came with each deep encounter with God. But the need for the active though always graced effort at ongoing conversion and real-life transformation is a consistent theme of Christian spirituality and growth in prayer since the beginnings of Christian living.

Most fundamental, Teresa of Avila and John of the Cross were recommending what modern writers continue to recommend for today's spiritual guides: try humbly and faithfully to be of assistance and offer what you can to help the person to become more attentive to God's action and direction and more free to respond wholeheartedly. The pursuit of such inner freedom often involves assistance in avoiding or overcoming self-deceit, encouragement through periods of dryness in prayer and challenges in the course of the Christian journey, and offering other perspectives that might serve to enlighten their experience. This might involve prudent questions and observations by the director or mention of how spiritual teachers in the past or in contemporary literature have responded in similar circumstances. Beyond that, together with modern writers on spiritual direction, both Teresa and John firmly believe that the human guide must simply get out of the way.

I have acknowledged throughout this text that the reflections on spiritual direction offered by Teresa of Jesus and John of the Cross must be understood within the context of the very different culture in which they lived. And yet, at the same time, I have sought to highlight how their fundamental insights have lasting value for a contemporary understanding of spiritual guidance in our own day. I trust that the reader who has engaged the longer quotations that have been included from their works has gained insights and counsel well beyond Teresa's and John's comments on the specific characteristics of a good guide. I conclude now by offering some summary remarks about the ongoing value, in particular, of the three essential qualities of a good spiritual director that they advocated.

The Director as Learned

To say that a spiritual director must be "learned," in our day, would seem to say that a reliable guide must have advanced academic degrees. Surely, this is not always the case. But we can see why it was important to Teresa and John. Their basic insight is still recognized in the fact that formation programs for spiritual directors generally include an academic component in which the Scriptures, theology, and spirituality are studied in order to equip spiritual guides with important resources to enhance their ministry. In my own academic institution, a master's degree in a theological discipline or completion of a permanent deacon formation program is required as a prerequisite for admission to the certificate program in spiritual direction. And the formation requirements include courses in the history of Christian spirituality, spiritual themes in Scripture, dimensions of human development, and the theology and history of spiritual direction and discernment. Such study is only one component of forming good spiritual directors, of course, but an essential part of it. The Christian community and its long tradition have vast resources to offer persons—and those who walk with them—as they discern God's will and seek growth in deeper prayer and in an even more authentic Christian living. At its best, such knowledge must also be nurtured and enlightened by a deeper wisdom that comes as a gift from God to persons of prayer.

Becoming "learned" for a spiritual guide of today, of course, is not a one-time accomplishment but an ongoing journey. Professionals in every field recognize the need for continuing education and reading. This is no less true in the art of spiritual direction. Continued reading about spiritual direction, spirituality, prayer, psychology, and other disciplines is essential so that she or he can continue to "bring out treasures both old and new" (Matt 13:52) for the benefit of the person who comes for guidance. Continued prayerful encounter and study of the Word of God is simply essential for one who seeks to help others to discern the movement and action of God's Spirit in their distinctive Christian journey.

The Director as Experienced

In our day, to speak of an "experienced" director is to suggest experience in offering direction—and, again, formation programs for directors do generally require some type of formal mentoring in its practice. Teresa and John write little about fostering wise experience in the art of direction itself. In a real sense, they are themselves the experienced directors—as well as being experienced in being directed—who are seeking to mentor those who read their works. (Recall the comment of

Thomas Green, SJ, cited earlier, that he annually rereads John of the Cross's teaching on spiritual direction from the *Living Flame of Love* to serve as a kind of check of his own practice.) In our day, especially but not exclusively for those beginning direction, it is prudent to have a formal mentor or supervisor or at least a more experienced director(s) who can offer sound counsel in the practice of accompanying others along the way.

But Teresa's and John's fundamental insistence on the personal experience of the director as a person of faith and prayer remains true in every age. Surely anyone seeking spiritual guidance from another expects that the guide will have a deep and mature Christian faith and sustained personal experience in the practice of prayer, including varieties of methods and practices, common pitfalls, and traditional recommendations. If the Holy Spirit is the true director, then the human guide must know the Spirit and be accustomed to attending to the Spirit's movements and guidance in his or her own life—even while recognizing that the journey of the other person will never be exactly like one's own.

The Director as Discerning

The movement of the Holy Spirit and the call of God in our lives are often subtle. At the same time, each person has his or her own experience of and personal call from God. God relates to all of us individually, personally, and intimately. People are in different places in their lives. No two people can be guided in the exact same way, along the exact same path. And so, it makes perfect sense that a good spiritual director must be "discerning." This is a multidimensional reality. The guide must be able to assist the other to uncover the presence and movements of the Spirit in the life of the one guided. But this is true, as well, in the life of the guide, as he or she seeks to discern the appropriate response, question, word of encouragement or challenge, or suggestion to offer to the other.

But to call the good spiritual director "discerning" is also to speak of the virtue of prudence. In its natural form, this includes the ability to intuit the other person's unique need and actual situation as the guide listens in a particular moment. And it involves as well the director's ability to be self-critical (and open to the Spirit's challenge) about his or her own motivations that might be a hindrance rather than a help, any tendency to project a personal agenda into the relationship or conversation, and acceptance of his or her own limitations as a director, whether in general or in regard to this particular person who seeks accompaniment. And yet human prudence is aided as well by a divine gift that is traditionally called "infused" prudence—that is, the ability to intuit in at least a tentative way what a next step might be for this person who wants better to understand God's will, embrace it more deeply and broadly in daily life, or grow in a deeper relationship with God.

The Director Needs All Three

Teresa and John urged not just one but all three qualities—and not isolated and compartmentalized from one another. The three characteristics must be able to come together as needed in service of the one who seeks guidance. Discerning the most appropriate response at any particular moment involves the guide's ability to draw together her or his already acquired knowledge ("learning"), personal experience of God's action, and gifted prudence in order to help the other person to discern the call of the Spirit at this moment in life. The director's more conceptual knowledge about the Christian journey must be fed by personal encounter with God, yielding a deeper kind of intuitive, spiritual knowledge. At the same time, the guide's personal experience of God must seek the resources of the Christian tradition to be understood and made ready to share with others. Such knowledge and experience help to form a deeper discernment of the movements of the Holy Spirit.

Thomas Green, SJ, suggests in the title of a book on spiritual direction that the good spiritual director is a "friend of the Bridegroom."[1] Teresa of Avila and John of the Cross understood the deepening Christian life and prayer according to what has been called a "bridal," "spousal," or "love" mysticism. I suspect that they would resonate with Green's term. The good spiritual director is a friend of the Divine Bridegroom and, in a distinctive way, a friend of the one who comes for guidance. Spiritual direction is fundamentally a graced human relationship that serves and seeks to deepen a human relationship with the divine, lived in ordinary daily life. Teresa and John clearly believed that anyone called to this special service of love should possess and actively seek to grow in knowledge, experience, and discernment to serve well.

1. Thomas H. Green, *The Friend of the Bridegroom: Spiritual Direction and the Encounter with Christ* (Notre Dame, IN: Ave Maria Press, 2000).

Bibliography

Spiritual Direction

Barry, William A., and William J. Connolly. *The Practice of Spiritual Direction*. 2nd ed. New York: HarperOne, 2009.

Benner, David G. *Sacred Companions: The Gift of Spiritual Friendship and Direction*. Downers Grove, IL: InterVarsity Press, 2002.

Edwards, Tilden. *Spiritual Director, Spiritual Companion: Guide to Tending the Soul*. New York: Paulist Press, 2001.

Green, Thomas H. *The Friend of the Bridegroom: Spiritual Direction and the Encounter with Christ*. Notre Dame, IN: Ave Maria Press, 2000. (Chapter 4: "St. John of the Cross and the Danger of the 'Blind Guide,'" 71–90.)

Louf, André. *Grace Can Do More: Spiritual Accompaniment and Spiritual Growth*. Translated by Susan Van Winkle. Kalamazoo, MI: Cistercian Publications, 2002.

Merton, Thomas. *Spiritual Direction and Meditation*. Collegeville, MN: Liturgical Press, 1960.

Mulloor, Augustine, and Johnson Perumittath, eds. *To Be Effective Carmelite Spiritual Directors: Relearning from Carmelite Spiritual Resources*. Rome, Italy: Casa Generalizia de Carmelitani Scalzi, 2014.

Ranft, Patricia. *A Woman's Way: The Forgotten History of Women Spiritual Directors*. New York: Palgrave, 2000.

Ruffing, Jane. *Uncovering Stories of Faith*. New York: Paulist Press, 1989.

Smith, Gordon T. *Spiritual Direction: A Guide to Giving and Receiving Direction*. Downers Grove, IL: InterVarsity Press, 2014.

Teresa of Avila

Álvarez-Suárez, Aniano. "Acompañamiento espiritual." In *Diccionario de Santa Teresa*, edited by Tomás Álvarez, 16–21. 2nd ed. Burgos, Spain: Editorial Monte Carmelo, 2006.

Arias Luna, Juanito. *El acompañamiento espiritual a los jóvenes desde Santa Teresa en sus dos obras de Vida y Moradas*. Quito, Ecuador: Editorial Iberia, 2015.

Giallanza, Joel. "Spiritual Direction According to St. Teresa of Avila." In *Spiritual Direction: Contemporary Readings*, edited by Kevin Culligan, 203–11. Locust Valley, NY: Living Flame Press, 1983.

González, María Trinidad. "Dirección espiritual y transformación interior en Santa Teresa de Jesús." STL thesis, Universidad Pontificia Comillas de Madrid, Instituto de Teología Espiritual, 2006.

Kanjiramukkil, Datius. "Spiritual Direction in the Teaching and Example of St. Teresa." In *To Be Effective Carmelite Spiritual Directors: Relearning from Carmelite Spiritual Resources*, edited by Augustine Mulloor and Johnson Perumittath, 55–10. Rome, Italy: Casa Generalizia de Carmelitani Scalzi, 2014.

Lépée, Marcel. "Spiritual Direction in the Letters of St. Teresa." In *Carmelite Studies I: Spiritual Direction*, edited by John Sullivan, 61–80. Washington, DC: ICS Publications, 1980.

O'Reilly, Terence. "St. Teresa and her First Jesuit Confessors." In *St. Teresa of Ávila: Her Writings and Life*, edited by Terence O'Reilly, Colin P. Thompson, and Lesley Twomey, 108–23. Studies in Hispanic and Lusophone Cultures 19. Cambridge, England: Legenda (Modern Humanities Research Association), 2018.

John of the Cross

Álvarez-Suárez, Aniano. "Dirección espiritual." In *Diccionario de San Juan de la Cruz*, edited by Eulogio Pacho, 331–41. Burgos, Spain: Editorial Monte Carmelo, 2009.

———. "Discreción." In *Diccionario de San Juan de la Cruz*, edited by Eulogio Pacho, 341–42. Burgos, Spain: Editorial Monte Carmelo, 2009.

Casero, José. "El Espíritu Santo agente principal en la dirección de alma: estudio a partir de San Juan de la Cruz." *Teología espiritual* 23 (May–August 1979): 131–80.

Culligan, Kevin. "Qualities of a Good Guide: Spiritual Direction in John of the Cross' Letters." In *Carmelite Studies VI: John of the Cross*, edited by Steve Payne, 65–83. Washington, DC: ICS Publications, 1992.

———. "Toward a Model of Spiritual Direction Based on the Writings of Saint John of the Cross and Carl Rogers: An Exploratory Study." PhD diss., Boston University Graduate School, 1979.

D'Souza, Gregory. "Spiritual Direction in the Life and Writings of St. John of the Cross." In *To Be Effective Carmelite Spiritual Directors: Relearning from Carmelite Spiritual Resources*, edited by Augustine Mulloor and Johnson Perumittath, 105–59. Rome, Italy: Casa Generalizia de Carmelitani Scalzi, 2014.

Florent, Lucien-Marie. "Spiritual Direction According to St. John of the Cross." In *Carmelite Studies I: Spiritual Direction*, edited John Sullivan, 3–34. Washington, DC: ICS Publications, 1980.

Gabriel of St. Mary Magdalene. *The Spiritual Director According to the Principles of St. John of the Cross*. Westminster, MD: Newman Press, 1952.

Giallanza, Joel. "Spiritual Direction According to St. John of the Cross." In *Spiritual Direction: Contemporary Readings*, edited by Kevin Culligan, 196–202. Locust Valley, NY: Living Flame Press, 1983.

Graviss, Dennis. *Portrait of the Spiritual Director in the Writings of Saint John of the Cross*. 2nd rev. ed. Rome, Italy: Edizioni Carmelitane, 2014.

Hódar Maldonado, Manuel. *San Juan de la Cruz, guía de maestros espirituales: meta, camino, y guía del místico.* Burgos, Spain: Editorial Monte Carmelo, 2009.

Tyler, Peter M. *St. John of the Cross*. New York: Continuum, 2010. (Chapter 7: "John for Today: Pastoral Theologian and Spiritual Director," 143–52.)